Father, Can You Teach Me How to Live?

FATHER, CAN YOU TEACH ME HOW TO LIVE?

Father, Can You Teach Me How to Live?

By Kathleen Alford

LITTLE BIRD PUBLICATIONS

ISBN: 978-16-92789-05-3

Never would I have thought that I'd find a spiritual director in Central America. But I had asked—I had begged—the Blessed Virgin Mary to help me. Why? So many reasons! Too many to list here, but I will tell you some of them in the following pages. And I will tell you something else: If you consecrate yourself to Jesus through Mary, you will never regret having done it.

For Father Jeffry, who taught me how

to live a joyful life.

a/k/a

Don't worry! Be happy!

FATHER, CAN YOU TEACH ME HOW TO LIVE?

CONTENTS

FATHER, CAN YOU TEACH ME HOW TO LIVE?

CHAPTER 1

How It All Began

a/k/a

Father, Can You Teach Me How to Live?

I MET FATHER JEFFRY MOORE in Costa Rica while my husband, George, and I were vacationing there one February a few years ago. George had made Fr. Jeffry's acquaintance the year before on a surfing trip with his buddies, and he was determined that I should meet this priest. Arrangements were made to have dinner together in Tamarindo, located about 20 minutes from our cabin in Avellanas.

I made up my mind to be friendly and conversational during dinner despite my inner awkwardness at meeting new people in social situations. I need not have worried. It turned out that Father Jeffry was outgoing and genial enough for both of us! Indeed, the talk and camaraderie during dinner was so relaxed and interesting that I barely noticed what we were eating. At one point I asked Father Jeffry, "What do you find to be the best thing about being a priest?"

"Hearing confessions," he replied. I blinked in surprise. I guess he noticed my look of astonishment because he went on to explain. "Hearing confessions is where I think I can do the most good." I noticed his warmth and caring as he spoke and his genuine desire to bring healing to people who were struggling under the weight of sin.

"Are you on Facebook?" he asked suddenly, breaking my concentration.

"Yes," I answered.

"We should become friends!" he exclaimed. "Here, let me have your phone." Father Jeffry reached his hand across the table, and I meekly turned over my phone to him. I had never met a priest like this before. I didn't know what to make of him. It took him only seconds to finish and hand my phone back to me. "There, now we're friends," he said, as if this transaction had been the most natural thing in the world.

I watched him more closely during the rest of dinner. I figured he must be in his late 50's or early 60's, a big man with short-cropped brown hair and dancing eyes. The restaurant's hostess obviously knew him and liked him, and George thought the world of him. I decided that I liked him, too, and I let down my customary guard.

When we left the restaurant, George offered to give Father Jeffry a lift to wherever he was staying, but he preferred to walk. So, we said goodnight and drove back to Avellanas. Later that night as I lay in bed, I mulled over what

Father Jeffry had said about the healing to be found in the Sacrament of Confession. A hunger to be free of the burdens I was carrying gnawed at my soul. I had been praying to the Blessed Virgin Mary for help in my spiritual life. Could Father Jeffry be her answer to my prayer? The longing for inner peace grew until I could resist it no longer. I reached for my phone and messaged my new Facebook friend.

"Father, I do not have mortal sins," I typed, *"but I am weighed down with other sins that I don't know how to deal with. May I come to you for confession?"* I pressed the blue arrow, nervously wondering what he would say.

"Absolutely!" he messaged back. We worked out the details, and then I talked to George to confirm the arrangements. We would meet him in Tamarindo the next day at 5:00 p.m.

The following afternoon Father Jeffry heard my confession under a shady tree by the beach in Tamarindo. He spent an hour with me listening, asking questions, and giving guidance. I told him everything, even more than I had planned, and I was glad I did. He taught me with authority, illustrating his points with such clarity that I knew what was right and what to do. Before giving me absolution, he asked me to pray a decade of the rosary for penance. "That will be easy," I said. "I pray the rosary every day."

"This is in addition to that," he replied, his tone serious. "Penance is to be done in reparation, to repair the damage. Sin hurts our relationship with God. It's not up to us to say, 'Oh, that sin was only a trifle to you.' *All* sin hurts our relationship with God."

"Yes, Father," I replied softly. He then asked me to pray a good Act of Contrition. After I did, he prayed over me and absolved me of my sins.

I won't share my confession here, but I will share some of what Father Jeffry taught me during this confession:

- There is no reincarnation. Each person is brought into existence and will be judged by Jesus. He will judge fairly and with mercy.
- Gossip is to be avoided at all costs. It is like a knife in the back. What you said will get out, and that person will hear it.
- It is okay for parents to "vent" to each other regarding childrearing, as long as love for the child is always affirmed at the end of the conversation.
- When tempted toward resentment, maintain an attitude of mercy, saying, "I will not judge."
- Pray for adult children as St. Monica prayed for St. Augustine, but remember that adult children stand on their own two feet and are responsible for their own decisions.
- Never be afraid to go to confession. Priests have heard it all. They don't try to remember or dwell on a penitent's sins. They respect you for confessing.

I thought once we left Costa Rica, I would never see Father Jeffry again. Thankfully, I was wrong. But just in case, I tentatively decided to message him a question: *What do you call the Blessed Mother when you talk to her? Every way I try to address her seems either too distant or too familiar. Anyway, I'm just wondering if you have a way to address her that feels right to you.*

He answered, *Mother.*

I will try that, I replied.

Next day: *Well, I tried it. It didn't feel too distant or too formal, but I felt awkward. Though I am a mother and grandmother many times over, the whole concept of "being mothered" feels awkward. I guess I still look at her at Jesus' mother, not mine. The Consecration to Mary that I made four years ago feels like a contract with her. And I work for her as Jesus' mother, but not mine.*

He sent a picture:

> Magdalen. 26When Jesus therefore had seen his mother and the disciple standing whom he loved, he saith to his mother: Woman, behold thy son. 27After that, he saith to the disciple: Behold thy mother. And from that hour, the disciple took her to his own.

Then he added, *When Jesus told John, "Behold thy mother, she was given to mankind as mother.*

I messaged back, *I have read that verse before, but Jesus really only said that to John, right? And so maybe Jesus was just making sure she had a home and would be taken care of after He died. But I do remember watching a DVD about Our Lady of Guadalupe where she said to St. Juan Diego, 'Am I not here who am your mother?' Maybe calling her 'Mother' feels awkward because I am resisting her authority over me.*

Father Jeffry replied, *Jesus gave her to us for our own good. Even now He answers her prayers because He is true to His own law, which is to honor your father and your mother.*

The thought of Jesus being obedient to his parents gave me pause. I was used to thinking of him as Savior and King, victorious over death, not as an obedient Son who had set an example for me to follow.

When next I came to prayer, I approached Mary in an attitude of a daughter's obedience and found that calling her "Mother" no longer felt awkward. It felt right.

A few days later, George and I arrived back home in Florida. I felt more alive spiritually than I had in a very long time, and I felt a new sense of hope that questions hidden in my heart might be answered—that is, if I had the courage to ask them. I wondered if Father Jeffry would continue to respond to my messages, since I was no longer in his area of the world. Priests are so busy! Would he have time to type online answers to my questions? Or would my persistence a be nuisance to him and a hindrance to his ministry? Thankfully, he made time to write back to me!

One morning I sent him a question by Facebook Messenger and was stunned to discover that he was no longer in Costa Rica! No, he was in Orlando, less an hour away from my house! When I asked if we could come and visit him, he welcomed the idea. And so, we arrived at the place where he was staying on a Tuesday morning in April, about two months after our initial meeting in Costa Rica.

"It is a miracle that you are here!" I announced joyfully, barely able to contain myself from jumping up and down in delight. Father Jeffry had come out of the house to greet my husband and me, and he smiled broadly at my exuberance. "Why don't we walk by the lake?" he suggested. I had messaged him that I hoped to go to confession before Easter. Allowing penitents to walk while confessing seemed to be his modus operandi, and curiously, it did make it easier for me to say what was on my mind. A hot Florida sun shone brightly on us as we walked.

"Father," I began my confession, as we started around the lake. "I don't take very good care of my health. I spend a lot of my waking hours being frustrated and angry inside myself, and so I frequently run out of patience with other people and even with God." I paused and then asked, "Father, can you teach me how to live?"

"What do you mean?" he asked, seeking clarification, but looking straight ahead as we walked.

The words spilled out. "I don't know how to balance work and family life. I don't know where to draw the line between taking care of other people and taking care of myself. I can't ever seem to get enough sleep. I never seem to have enough time to split between my husband, my children, my tutoring business, and the ministries I'm involved in at church." I took a breath. "I just don't know how to make life work."

"Okay," he said. Then he asked, "How much sleep do you get?"

"What?"

"How much sleep do you get every night?" he repeated.

I shrugged. "I don't know. It all depends."

"On what?"

"On how much work there is to be done."

"On average, how much?" he persisted.

"Maybe four or five hours," I admitted, "but if there's a lot of work, then maybe only three."

"That's not good," Father Jeffry commented. "This is what you are to do: You are to set a time to wake up every day. Make some coffee when you get up, and then pray Morning Prayer. Start the day with Jesus. Look forward to it. Stay in bed until it's time to get up."

I was nearly incredulous. *"Stay in bed?"*

"Um-hmm. Set a time to go to sleep each night, so that you get adequate sleep," he added. "And do *not* stay up all night reading." Previously I had told him in a message that I had been up all night reading a really good book. He had made no comment at that time, so now I was surprised that he remembered.

However, I was even more surprised to be told I had to go to bed at the same time every night and stay in bed until it was time to get up. "Father, I have *never* done that in my whole life! This would be a *major* change for me!" I stared at the ground as we padded along the grassy bank of the lake in silence. Inside I felt desperate—nearly in tears—

at the thought of having a regular bedtime. "How much sleep do I have to get?" I asked.

"That's up to you," he answered. "Set the times and stick with it."

"But what if I have work that I have to do?" I pleaded.

He didn't budge. "There is work that *must* be done, and then there is 'busy work'. Not everything has to be done *now*. Work isn't meant to be done all at once."

My heart sank. I could hardly believe Father Jeffry was directing me to do this—to sleep—as the first step of learning how to live.

He had told me a while back that it was up to me whether to accept his direction or not. He would not be upset with me either way. It was up to me. Would I do it?

"Okay, Father, I will start tonight."

"Good girl," he said, and he smiled.

We talked about other issues that day, but being told to sleep made the deepest impression on me. At the end of my confession, Father Jeffry requested that I pray as my penance the Divine Mercy Chaplet on Good Friday, which was only three days away. He asked me for a good Act of Contrition, and after I prayed it aloud, he absolved me.

On the drive home, I was pensive. After a lifetime of disobedience and neglect regarding sleep, could I now suddenly become compliant? Would I be able to turn over a new leaf with the snap of a finger, or rather, with a Sign of the Cross? Inside myself I sulked like a child sent to her room.

My doctor had told me he wanted me to get at least seven hours of sleep every night in order to reduce the toll that stress was taking on my body. *Impossible!* I had thought at the time. But now?

When I got home, I did some research on the daily schedule of Mother Teresa of Calcutta, whom I considered to be a modern-day Catholic heroine. At that time, I was reading a book about her, entitled *Mother Teresa, CEO,* by Ruma Bose and Lou Faust, and I figured that as hard as she worked for the poorest of the poor, she probably didn't sleep that much. However, her schedule in the book indicated that Mother Teresa of Calcutta went to bed every night at about 10 p.m., and she was in the chapel for prayer by 5 a.m. I also found an article online at http://www.philipkosloski.com/saints-daily-schedules/ that agreed approximately with these times for rising and retiring.

I messaged Father Jeffry, including the link to the article I had just read. *What if I set my alarm for 5 a.m. and lights out at 10 p.m.? That's seven hours of sleep, like Mother Teresa. Is that okay?*

You have to set your times and live by them," he answered cryptically, neither agreeing nor disagreeing.

I sighed in resignation. *Then I'm going to try 5 a.m. and 10 p.m. for wake-up and bedtime, respectively, but this is a big change, Father. I have been undisciplined about sleep my whole life. I got* spanked regularly as a child for getting out of bed, yelled at as a teenager, advised by doctors, worried over by my husband, all to no avail. I do want to obey Our Lord in this, though, and I did ask Jesus to teach me how to live. I get it that this is His will for me. Please pray for me to follow through.

His reply was firm. *You'll think of a hundred reasons why to change, but don't. You'll have no problem getting up, I am sure. Getting to bed may be harder. Remember that you are sometimes able to appreciate things and sometimes not. Imagine going to a concert of an orchestra and you are very tired. You will sleep through the concert and not enjoy it. That is why you have to be rested and ready to go to the concert to appreciate it. It is the same thing with prayer. Enjoy that time in bed until the alarm rings. Do not be tempted to be "more productive."*

How well he knew the pitfalls of my human nature! *"The temptation to increase productivity"* was exactly the pull that would be hard to resist.

The next day I messaged him to report how it went, but when he asked, *Well, how was your sleep schedule? According to plan?* I hesitated a moment before telling him the truth.

Might as well spit it out. *Lights out at 9:56 after moving my books to avoid the temptation to stay up and read. I prayed a rosary. I fell asleep at 12:30 a.m. Woke up around 3 a.m. Fell asleep again around 3:30 and stayed asleep until the alarm went off at 5:00. That's only four hours of sleep, and I know that's not good. But it's better than I would have gotten before because I would have gotten up at 3 if you hadn't told me to stay in bed until the alarm,* I concluded. Then I added, *And I had a really wonderful first hour of the day with Jesus at 5:00.*

Then SUCCESS! he exclaimed. *To stay in bed until the alarm was the biggest goal.*

Much relieved, I took a big breath and typed, *One of the reasons I stay up late is to have quiet time after everyone else is asleep. But the quiet time was much better in the morning. I had my coffee and prayed Morning Prayer and read a section from both books I'm reading. It was very peaceful. I am looking forward to it again tomorrow. And maybe I won't take so long to fall asleep tonight. Thank you so much, Father.*

After lunch came the afternoon dip in energy and customary drowsiness. "I need more coffee," I said aloud. But then I wondered what Father Jeffry would say about that. After all, drinking too much coffee during the afternoon supposedly kept people from sleeping restfully at night. I decided that he if was online, it wouldn't hurt to check.

Father Jeffry, I am falling asleep at my computer. Should I have more coffee or not?

Coffee! he replied enthusiastically, and then he added, *But a nap is sooo good!*

I blinked. *You think I should take a* nap?

Didn't you read that in Mother Teresa's schedule? he asked. *She took a nap every day.*

No way! I *didn't* remember seeing that. I didn't remember that *at all!* I had to check it out for myself.

I searched the article again. Sure enough, there it was right in the middle of her daily schedule: "12:30-2:30 Lunch and rest".

I clicked back on the conversation with Father Jeffry. He had typed, *You checked, didn't you?*

Yes, Father, I admitted. *I guess I'll go take a nap then.*

Just for a half hour. Otherwise you won't sleep tonight.

5:00-6:30 Prayers and Mass
6:30-8:00 Breakfast and cleanup
8:00-12:30 Work for the poor
12:30-2:30 Lunch and rest
2:30-3:00 Spiritual reading and meditation
3:00-3:15 Tea break
3:15-4:30 Adoration
4:30-7:30 Work for the poor
7:30-9:00 Dinner and clean

Okay, I will set my alarm for a half hour.

Sweet dreams! he said.

Outfoxed, I put my phone down and headed to my bedroom. I hated taking naps! From my earliest memories I had always hated taking naps. Why? Because I hardly ever fell asleep! Instead, I stared at the ceiling in agonizing boredom until either I sneaked out of bed or until someone let me out of jail. Surprisingly, though, I did fall asleep that day. And I felt good when I woke up. I still got some more coffee after my nap, just the same.

In a few weeks, I experienced the fruit of obedience: my first full night of seven hours' sleep without interruption! I was amazed to be able to fall asleep soon after putting my head on the pillow and waking up rested at 5:00.

That ended Round 1 of "The Battle of the Bed", but the war within was far from over. As my work started backing up, I grew increasingly uneasy. It was one thing to have a set bedtime and to get up at the same time every day; it was quite another to figure out how to prioritize what I should be doing during my waking hours. That, however, would be among many other lessons to come in learning how to live.

Thus began what became more than two years of spiritual guidance and teaching by Father Jeffry on dozens of topics, mostly via the Internet, especially Facebook Messenger and email. In the process, Father Jeffry taught me how to live a holy, worry-free life filled with health, happiness, joy, and purpose.

From here on out, please feel free NOT to read this book in order, but to skip around and read the lessons that interest you most. Whatever your question about the spiritual life, I bet Father Jeffry has addressed it in some form at one time or another. No matter in which order you decide to explore, I pray that you enjoy the journey and that you benefit from having perused these pages.

CHAPTER 2

Adoring Jesus

a/k/a

Do's and Don'ts in the Adoration Chapel

Question: Good morning, Father Jeffry. I'm writing you from the Adoration Chapel. I entered into the silence of the Blessed Mother, as I was advised to do by the priest in confession. I was surprised how painful it was! What came up in my heart were thoughts of mistrust and resentment toward Mother Mary because of some incidents that happened recently. I don't understand why she let these things happen. Is it okay for me to ask you about this?

Father Jeffry: Children sometimes get mad at their parents because of what they do to the children, like restricting their freedom. However, as you know from experience, the parents see the big picture and understand what they are doing.

I have a question for you, and it seems now is the time to

ask it politely. You said that you are writing me from the Adoration Chapel. It would seem to me important to only adore Jesus in the Eucharist when you are there and that no communication with anyone should impinge on the time set aside for Him. It was once said by a holy man, "It is better to talk to God about men than to talk to men about God."

Reply: But Father, it is hard to sit still and be quiet and not do anything else. Most of the time when I go to the chapel, I pray Morning Prayer or a rosary or an Our Lady of Sorrows rosary or read or journal. When He tells me to sit still and be quiet--He has told me that before, too--part of me wants to run away, which is strange since I went to the chapel to be with Jesus in the first place. Tomorrow, though, if the Holy Spirit tells me to sit still and be quiet, I will, even though I don't understand why He wants me to do it.

I know there's a verse that says, "Be still and know that I am God," and I can do that for a couple of minutes without getting squirmy, but not much more than that. Even when I entered into the silence of Mary in my mind and heart, my body was still busy doing something else. I have just never been good at being still. How do you do it, Father? How do you make yourself be still?

Father Jeffry: Being still before God is not to be thought of as a chore; it is rather a hope that some of that perpetual light will shine through and also some of that Eternal Love. We all want to be loved and it really feels good in big doses. Well, God takes advantage of quiet moments because it is only when you are quiet that you can really hear Him because you don't have the white noise interfering in your thoughts. He speaks clearly when we are disposed to listen to him. I used to read a small paragraph of the Bible and meditate on it and pray about what I learned. That is a healthy way to spend your time. Do not take an iPad or a phone with you. If anyone needs you, they will know where to find you. Your time dedicated to the Most Sacred Heart will be rewarded in Heart-to-heart spiritual conversations.

Reply (*the next evening*): So, Father, I didn't take my phone into the chapel this morning. I sat down on a chair, determined to sit still, be quiet, and do whatever the Holy Spirit told me to do. The first thing that happened was the sense that it was quite all right for me to sit cross-legged on the floor where I am comfortable, so I moved to my usual spot on the floor near the tabernacle.

I looked up at Jesus in the monstrance and waited. I was steeling myself in case I didn't hear anything because there have been plenty of times when I have desperately wanted to hear His voice and heard nothing at all, no matter how hard I listened. For a minute or two, there was nothing, but then I felt invited to start, as if Jesus said, "So, talk to me," but without words. I pulled out my journal and wrote Him the question that was on my mind: "What should I cook for the retreat?" And then lots of answers came! And it felt like it wasn't only Jesus, but Mother Mary, too, and the Holy Spirit, too, and maybe others! I wrote it all down, and these became the menus for the weekend. By then it was only 5:30 or so. I didn't hear anything else. But then it felt like the Holy Spirit invited me to open the new book on Mary, *Stepping on the Serpent*. I had brought my book, but I didn't think I would get to read it.

I read the introduction. It was all about how we learn to trust Jesus best through companionship with Mary, and how the author would show us the way. At the end of the introduction, Fr. Thaddeus Lancton said to read his poem as if the Lord Himself were speaking directly to me. When I read the poem, I felt Jesus asking me, *"Will you trust me?"* as He promised to love me and take care of me and lead me home to heaven. Father Jeffry, I read it with my heart wide open, and then I cried and gave Jesus all the trust I had.

You were so right about Jesus pouring out His love in the Blessed Sacrament!

Father Jeffry: Great to read this! Goodnight!

CHAPTER 3

A Question of Innocence

a/k/a

Nakedness Before God

Question: I have always thought that innocence means being perfect and sinless. I had never, ever thought of innocence as complete openness to God and complete trust in Him. It makes sense to me, though, after reflection, and it is a major relief to me! I will probably never be perfectly sinless or virtuous, but I can be completely open to God by choosing to trust him completely. I can do that, and so I will do that.

Father Jeffry: Great! If you were perfectly sinless and virtuous, you would not need a Savior.

Reply: I have thought more about the story of Adam and Eve, how they hid from God because they were afraid. But He wasn't going to hurt them! He must have been very sad to make them clothes, so that they could "hide" from Him at least partially. I take this to mean that God allows us to feel hidden from Him, so that we aren't afraid. But I am glad not to be hidden anymore, not one bit. I am completely open and uncovered to Him because I know He loves me and would never harm me. This "Him" is Jesus, yes--but the Father, too--and the Holy Spirit, who is always there!

Father Jeffry: Knowledge of good and bad. They came to know that their actions were bad because of disobedience. But the reality is that God re-creates us in Baptism and continues recreating us through the sacrament of Reconciliation. There is an ontological change which happens in Baptism; I would say in Reconciliation as well. There is a change not seen by human vision. There is a re-creation similar to an artist who is modeling clay. Imagine the clay slowly changing form and an arm sagging for example. The artist could insert something inside the clay to support his creation. That is what it is like with God and us. He always gives us what we need. But God respects His creation which is the freedom which he has given us, and that is different than respecting the person who is His creation. God is not a respecter of men.

Acts 10: And Peter opening his mouth, said: in very deed I perceive that God is not a respecter of persons. 3But in every nation, he that feareth him and worketh justice is acceptable to him.

CHAPTER 4

The Communion of Saints

a/k/a

Why Bother to Offer Up Sacrifices?

Question: I have been reading Peter Kreeft's book, *Everything You Ever Wanted to Know about Heaven But Never Dreamed of Asking!* My ears perked up immediately when I started listening to the chapter about "The Communion of Saints", which you had just talked about to me.

Father Jeffry: Peter Kreeft is a great and orthodox philosopher.

Reply: One thing the author explained in the chapter was why God asks us to learn to sacrifice for others. He said that "love" is the language of eternity and is the way of life in the Communion of Saints. I can't remember exactly how he put it, but the idea was that learning to sacrifice for others makes more room in our hearts for God and for others--for love! Well, then, I'd better embrace the sacrifices that Jesus asks of me in my daily life, rather than trying to escape them or muttering under my breath, because I want to have LOTS of room for God in my heart, and I want to be able to love everyone in heaven tremendously!

Father Jeffry: EXACTLY

Reply: When we pray to Jesus and Mary and the saints and angels, can they hear us?

Father Jeffry: Of course they can hear us because we have the power to communicate as do they. God created us to communicate with Him and each other.

Reply: How can they do that if they aren't all around us?

Father Jeffry: Again, you are attributing a physical place to a spiritual reality.

Note: If you have ever wondered what the experience of heaven will be like, I highly recommend Everything You Ever Wanted to Know about Heaven But Never Dreamed of Asking! *by Peter Kreeft. It's available in paperback, Kindle, and audiobook.*

CHAPTER 5

How to Go to Confession

a/k/a

Confession from the Priest's Point of View

Question: How many times can I confess the same sin without it becoming insincere?

Father Jeffry: As many times as it happens. You have to realize that sin can be habitual. That is where fighting the good fight, as St. Paul says, comes in. Don't become complacent or dejected if the sin is repeated because that repetition indicates a weakness against which one must struggle and not abandon hope.

Also, don't worry about what anyone thinks about the frequency of your confessions. Go whenever you want. Pope St. John Paul II went every day.

To make it easier on you, just confess your sins correctly and get it over with. That is what the sacrament is about. What is important for the priest is that you confess your sins honestly and show remorse, and he will give you absolution.

Go to confession whenever it is convenient. Remember that confession is for confessing sins… it is not for spiritual direction. In and out in a relatively short time. It often happens that people do their spiritual direction in the confessional and that is very destructive because it causes problems for the others that are waiting in line to confess. Others get frustrated that it is taking so long and come to the conclusion that it is not confession, but spiritual direction. The confessional is not the place for that.

Here is a link to a prayer before confession to pray for your confessor: http://wdtprs.com/blog/2018/09/a-prayer-for-your-confessor-the-priest-to-whom-you-are-about-to-make-your-confession/

Reply (*at a later date*): I want to tell you about something, but I'm wondering if I'm allowed to tell you about it because it refers to something I had confessed to you in the Sacrament, and so maybe you wouldn't be allowed to talk about it, and so I should keep it to myself. I am confused about what to do.

Father Jeffry: You can talk with me about something that you confessed by telling me about it outside of confession. I can't bring up something I heard in a confession even if you confessed it to me.

You can tell me anything you want outside of confession.

CHAPTER 6

Too Easy of a Penance

a/k/a

What If I Deserved a Lot Worse than I Got?

Question: I went to confession on Friday. I kept it simple, but I confessed everything. The priest gave me only an Our Father for penance, and after I prayed a good Act of Contrition, he absolved me from my sins. I think I deserved a tougher penance than that.

Father Jeffry: You are the judge of your sins, and that is why we accuse ourselves of our sins and admit (judge ourselves to be guilty), but the priest is the judge of our repentance and penance. Trust him. If it seems too little, pile on whatever you may, and then compare your penance to the price paid by Jesus Himself, and see how far you get with that logic. Accept the penance without question, and add love to it, if you think it is too small.

CHAPTER 7

Caring for an Aging Parent

a/k/a

What to Do When Parent and Child Change Places

Question: I should talk to you about Mom. Today I asked her if she wanted to stay sitting on the couch or go to her room to lie down. She said, "I don't know." I said, "Whatever you want to do is fine." She cried, "I don't know! I don't know!" The afternoon was trying. Struggling to keep my voice steady, I said, "Mom, I am not the enemy. I am trying to help. I will take you in to rest now. If you need anything, push your alarm button, okay?" And I left. A couple of hours later, she pushed her button, and I went into her room to get her, and she was fine.

Father, none of this is the end of the world, you know? And I realize that she is elderly. It's just that it gets to me. I am so uncomfortable treating my mother like a toddler, but I guess I don't have a choice. Is that right, Father?

Father Jeffry: Yes! You have, for all intents and purposes, THE AUTHORITY! When your mother can't make up her mind, do it for her, and that will take a burden off of her. In her indecisiveness, you be her rock!

You make her decisions for her, all the while allowing her to believe that she is deciding to go to bed or to the couch, in the measure possible, perhaps suggesting that she sounds a little tired and a nap would do her good!

Or, have a seat and then go to take a nap in about 30 minutes. That way you actually have offered her both possibilities, yet one after another in an orderly and logical fashion.

Reply: Thank you, Father Jeffry. The idea of assuming authority and being her "rock" creates a different image and sense of mission than did the idea of treating her like an unruly toddler. I will take to heart what you have said and put it into practice.

Reply (*another day*): It always seems to me that the great saints are filled with joy to be caring for the sick and infirm, but I am not. I remember St. Francis kissing the leper and Mother Teresa caring for the poorest of the poor who were covered with maggots. What is WRONG with me? Why do I not feel the joy that the saints feel when they take care of the sick, but instead feel repulsed by gross substances and smells and procedures, unless I am taking care of children? Is my love so small? If so, how do I make it bigger?

Father Jeffry: What makes you think they weren't grossed out? If they weren't, there was no merit in what they had done. But remember, she changed your diapers too. Was she grossed out? Yes! It helps to be thankful!

CHAPTER 8

The Desire for Silence

a/k/a

What to Do About the Noise

Question: Something that has remained with me from Lent is the desire for silence in order to be at peace inside and to encounter God in that peace. Today has not been a day for silence, though--at least not until now. Students and family members have been in and out all day. I enjoy all of them, but I crave the silence, too.

Father Jeffry: Silence is important. God speaks in silence. However, I have lived in seminaries, rectories, universities, dormitories, schools etc. and I have had to adapt myself to the circumstances of the situation. My best friend from St. Thomas and also Switzerland once told me how difficult it was for him to study at home to prepare his lessons to teach in the seminary because his children were constantly playing and screaming and just being kids. He said he wanted the silence but was aware that he had a "vocation to noise!"

Reply: I would say I have a "vocation to noise", too, during the day. At least I always have the first hour of the morning for quiet prayer! ☺

◆ ◆ ◆

CHAPTER 9

Cremation

a/k/a

Is It Okay for Catholics to Be Cremated?

Question: Father Jeffry, I was reading Cardinal Sarah's book, and he was talking about death and mourning. He wrote that "materialistic man" transforms death into "a noisy, exhibitionistic spectacle, in soulless funeral parlors, in pagan crematoriums and morbid funeral urns." I was surprised that Cardinal Sarah is apparently against cremation. I know that the Catholic Church *used* to be against it, but I have seen urns at Catholic funerals in recent years. I don't know what to think about cremation for myself. What are your thoughts on this, Father? What do you think is the best thing to do?

Father Jeffry: Both my mother and father were cremated. You can't imagine how many people have been cremated over the years in Europe! It is just the way things have been going for such a long time. When I wrote the obituary for my mother, I wrote something like, "Having a firm belief in the Resurrection of the dead, Velda wished to be cremated." The problem in the past was that people thought that if you disrespect your body so much as to burn it and make it impossible for God to resurrect you, then you don't believe in the resurrection. We, through a maturation of the faith, realize that Christ will resurrect us and is not impeded by something like cremation. What about those who died at sea and were eaten by sharks? Those burned to death in fires, etc. Do we judge them to be lost eternally? No. So, as long as you believe in the resurrection, there is nothing to worry about!

CHAPTER 10

Nervousness with the Pastor

a/k/a

The Discomfort of Feeling Vulnerable

Question: I finally talked to my pastor today about a problem in the parish. He listened and said we should bring it to prayer. Then he closed by saying that I could come to him anytime and that I should never be afraid to talk to him. I thanked him and went home. I don't know why I get so nervous with him.

Father Jeffry: I would like to address the nervousness issue. One can feel nervous when one feels vulnerable. BUT... there is no reason for you to feel vulnerable. A priest is not your superior. He is your servant. Of course he is not one who is paid to do menial things, but to serve you and your family by bringing holiness through the sacraments and the preaching of the Word. You should see the priest as a friend with whom, even though there may be tension from time to time, you will be able to arrive at a charitable relationship with mutual respect for you, to whom God sent him to serve, and him, as one sent to serve with holiness and kindness. It is always important to be able to trust.

CHAPTER 11

Gluttony

a/k/a

Overeating in Modern Society

Question: I have an odd question. Gluttony is classified as a deadly sin, but nobody ever talks about it. Overeating seems to be a normal part of life in America. I have never considered the sin of gluttony seriously until yesterday because of something I heard. Would "mindless eating" when you are already full be considered "gluttony", or is that just scrupulosity?

Father Jeffry: Yes, eating when full is gluttony. Of course it depends on the situation, like if you are eating a full-course meal in a restaurant but get full halfway through, it would not be gluttony if you were expected to finish your meal.

Reply (*after prayer*): I have never confessed this sin before, but I have done it a lot as far as eating more after I know I'm full. When praying about it, I first thought to myself, "Well, I didn't know any better," but that isn't really true. I have felt the tug of the Holy Spirit before to stop eating; I just didn't do it. The last couple of days I have been aware--not obsessive, but aware--when I felt full, and I stopped eating. So, now I think that I probably have overeaten at suppertime more often than not. I am aware that temperance is a virtue that God asks of us, but how do I confess this, Father? This is a lifetime habit that I am bringing to Jesus for healing, and I don't want to end up rambling because I can't find the right words.

Father Jeffry: You say, "I accuse myself of the sin of gluttony." Then go to the next sin. Remember confession is NOT spiritual direction. Your confession is no less a good confession if you don't go into detail. Make it easy on yourself. Just list your sins. As some priests call them: popcorn confessions… pop, pop, pop!

CHAPTER 12

Womanhood

a/k/a

What a Girl Needs to Know from Her Father

Question: In the quiet, I have been considering-- wondering--what it would have been like to be raised by you during my teen years. I wonder what you would have done differently, how you would have disciplined me, what you would have taught me about human sexuality, what you would have expected of me in regards to school and work, how you would have nurtured my faith, and how you would have encouraged my growth and freedom.

Some of this I can surmise from our interactions over the last two years. You would have expected obedience and truth, and you would have expected me to keep my word to you. You would have looked for willing and knowledgeable cooperation, not fearful, ignorant subservience. Regarding discipline, you would have taught me the reasons why you set certain standards and expectations, and then you would have been consistent and fair. You probably would have established a bedtime, and you probably would not have let me be in so many clubs and officerships in high school because the added club work on top of college prep classes kept me up working late into the night. Still, I'm pretty sure that you would have given me a lot more freedom to explore life and to express myself.

Father Jeffry: I agree with the above. Right on not allowing so many extracurricular activities. Study is needed outside of class. Extracurricular activities steal time away. It is true that they do help build social skills and have many other benefits but there can be just too many things in a person's life!

In philosophy it is said, "Argument from authority is the weakest form of argumentation." Faith itself is believing when one doesn't have proof. But the question is… "Is it reasonable to believe?" What is desired is that a child or teenager accepts something because they see the light, not just because they were told by authority that they have to believe. We need these "AH HA!" moments! Then the object of faith assented to is truly assented to for life.

About human sexuality… Sex, in its perfection, is an expression of love. Sex, while expressing love is a giving of oneself. Sex can be giving; sex can be taking. Sex can be using another; sex can be building up of another. Sex can be sharing moments never to be forgotten; sex can be ugly and degrading. Sex is an expression of who God is. Sex can be HOLY. Sex should be HOLY. John Paul II said that sex between married couples is a sacrament because it is the reality of the Sacrament of Matrimony.

But most importantly sex is giving of oneself. That is why

foreplay can be so exciting because one is looking forward to what the other is offering… himself or herself!

Reply: You know how I told you I was turning away from thoughts that the Holy Spirit had said "no" to, and choosing instead to pick the joys of life? Well, yesterday my mind wandered to thinking about the fact that Jesus was a man anatomically, not just in his mind and emotions. (Weird, I know.) I was expecting the Holy Spirit to say "no" to thinking about that, but to my surprise, such was not the case. In fact, I started wondering why the Word that proceeds from God is male, unless God Himself is male. Jesus was begotten, not made, while Mary was made, not begotten. So then I wondered, what does that mean about being a woman? I have always loved being a woman, but does all of this mean that I am "less" than a man? I couldn't write you yesterday, so I decided to bring up the topic with George last night. If I understood him correctly, he said that God was "Father"--male. So again I wondered: What does this mean about my being a woman?

Father Jeffry: Nooooo!

Your value is your value in the eyes of God.

Let's look at it this way... God, as male created female. Wow! He created woman understanding that she can be the "help" for man, not in the sense of work, but rather in the sense of happiness. Women have extremely high esteem in the eyes of God.

Reply: Father, suppose just for a minute that I were your daughter in the flesh, instead of your spiritual daughter. What would you hope that I would become as a woman?

Father Jeffry: Mother and wife! These are the two most important things you personally could aspire to. Could you imagine where you would be without your husband and children? That's what life is about…giving life to others both physically and mentally!

Reply: And spiritually, too! Yes, Father, that is what I have loved most about being a woman: being a wife and mother, giving and nurturing life. Amid much sacrifice, this is where I have found my joy! And I know that you are right that my main vocation is to love George, physically and mentally, being kind to him and supporting him in every way that I can, and then to extend my love to everyone else in my life.

CHAPTER 13

Authenticity vs. Transparency

a/k/a

The Virtue of Being Cheerful Even When You Don't Feel Like it

Question: There is much talk these days about "transparency" and "authenticity" as being admirable and even virtuous. Yet, both you and Mother Teresa seem to indicate that one's outer demeanor need not--and perhaps *should* not--correspond to one's inner emotional or spiritual state.

So, I tried it this morning after Mass. Even though it is the one-year anniversary of my father's death and my mother is dragging and depressed, I decided to be bright and cheerful with everyone I talked to after Mass on the way to our cars in the parking lot and even with George when I came home. No one would have guessed how I was feeling inside. And it was good for them and for me!

I have family and close friends to whom I can reveal my inner feelings at the proper times, but not to just everyone and not all the time. My question is: What do I say to the voice that accuses me of being inauthentic and deceiving? Because it doesn't feel like that. It feels good and right. But I have not been able to shake this.

Father Jeffry: Authenticity has to do with your values. One should always strive to be honest, truthful, friendly, loving and most especially authentic. When a person loses their spouse, at the funeral home they smile and are kind to the people who took time to express their condolences. Of course they are sad inside, but one has to pull towards them the joys of life, like picking apples from a tree! You pick and bring them to yourself. As far as when I said that nobody has a right to know my inner thoughts and feelings, that is true unless I see fit to share them. One shares for a reason. You've heard the expression, "Familiarity breeds contempt." For that reason I wouldn't share things that I shouldn't with a spiritual directee. That is a curiosity that serves no good purpose.

Reply: What do I say to the voice that accuses me of being inauthentic and deceiving?

Father Jeffry: "Get behind me, Satan!" Take comfort in choosing the high road where there is no fear of future conflicts or revelation of insincerity.

CHAPTER 14

Fear of Rejection

a/k/a

What If God Doesn't Want My Love?

Question: What will it take for me to stop hiding from God, to stop feeling afraid that He will reject my love and my desire to please Him? I have no idea what it will take.

Father Jeffry: Well, I would say that nobody wants to show their darker side, their faults and shortcomings. In marriage, that is what is so great about having someone who loves you in spite of your shortcomings. Being loved anyway. It's like a marriage, you have to risk yourself. Entrust yourself to the other IN GIVING YOURSELF AS A GIFT TO THE OTHER. The reality of Christianity is GIVING and in giving ourselves we become the gift. Of course we want our gift to be accepted and appreciated. As it is with Jesus, so it is with us. He is gift to us; we are gifts to others. Whereas in marriage we say, I take thee (not really wrong but rather bold by today's standards), the couple should say I welcome you into my heart to be flesh of my flesh. That is what Jesus wants of us. That is why He actually gives us His flesh so that we become Him… divinized. Made Holy, made truly Christian.

CHAPTER 15

Missing the Presence of God

a/k/a

Living by Faith vs. Feelings

Question: Lately I don't hear Jesus or feel His presence, not even in Holy Communion. You have told me before that "feelings" aren't the important thing about prayer or the spiritual life. So, I am being faithful, no matter whether I hear or feel Him with me or not. I just don't understand why I don't sense Him. He can't be far. I miss Him.

Father Jeffry: Years ago my spiritual director told us of a story of a young monk who joined the monastery, knowing that his vocation was to be a monk and live in relative silence, prayer, and work. He went through what is comparable to, or perhaps was, the "Dark Night of the Soul". The question was of the merit attributable to this monk because this particular monk had no consolation in his soul. He felt no presence of God, he felt no joy of being united to God mystically or anything that would give him reason to continue through a "feeling" that he might have had. No, this poor guy was as arid as a desert. NOTHING in the way of any consolation from God, no voice of God speaking to him in his heart that no one else could hear. No, he lived the monastic life as dry as the sand in the desert. But his obstinacy in continuing his vocation in spite of the lack of consolation was, in fact, not a saving grace but rather the most perfect example of FAITH.

We believe in the Most Holy Trinity as a matter of FAITH! We do not believe on the condition that God gives me good feelings in my soul so that it makes my FAITH journey easier. No… We believe. That is it. We believe based on whether or not it is REASONABLE to believe or not. That reasonableness of our belief has nothing to do with feelings. Therefore, feeling good that God or Mary talks to you must be independent of your faith; in fact, a simple belief based on propositions of the faith are sufficient reason to believe and continue to believe.

CHAPTER 16

Restlessness

a/k/a

What to Do When the Grass Is Greener

Question: My better self knows that true joy lies in doing God's will and fulfilling the duties of my present state in life, not in escapist behavior. Father Jeffry, what do I need to do that I am not doing in order to stay on an even keel, quell the unrest within, and be at peace?

Father Jeffry: First of all, you are doing what you should do... recognize that there is a temptation to unrest. But you know that there is a tendency, as you said, to end up in trouble. The antidote is to counter the temptation by attaching the will to what is good, that stability to live one's vocation at home in tranquility. You just say to yourself, "I want to stay at home and live right and be happy!"

CHAPTER 17

Sleep Revisited

a/k/a

Rationalizing Rebellion

Question: I didn't write you yesterday because of what I did the night before. Last night I was in bed by 10 and got up this morning at 5, but the night before I slept from 10:30pm to 3am. I thought the clock had said 5:00, even though the alarm hadn't sounded, so I got up and got dressed for the day. By the time I noticed on my phone that it was 3:15, not 5:15, I thought it would be ridiculous to go back to bed once I was already dressed. Besides, I thought, maybe God wanted me to get up and start the day early. Thus, I reasoned myself into disobedience. I didn't feel bad about it until I received Holy Communion at Mass.

I didn't feel the tiredness yesterday because I always get an adrenaline rush from waking up early and pushing hard, but today I am tired as my body catches up. I'm sorry that I talked myself into doing what I knew was not good for my health and for disobeying yet again what I know God wants me to do regarding getting proper sleep.

I know that you said you would never be angry with me for disobeying you, but I am still feeling very sorry and small and quiet for doing what I knew inside was wrong.

I plan to go to confession on Saturday, but Father Jeffry, would you forgive me, too, please?

Father Jeffry: Yes, of course I forgive you!!!

Reply: Thank you, Father!

◆ ◆ ◆

CHAPTER 18

Having Fun

a/k/a

The Cure for "All Work and No Play"

Question: Can you teach me how to have fun? I notice that you have all sorts of fun with lots of people, but it is very rare that I do that. There always seems to me to be so much that needs to be done in the world.

Father Jeffry: First of all, it is important to understand that play is necessary for the growth of the person and the soul. We know that children learn how to interact with others through play. They learn to share, and they learn about justice and rights and ugliness (when fighting over toys). We see the joy of children when playing because they are having fun. I had a friend who was on a date with the daughter of one of his philosophy professors and he was a bit nervous and realized that he had to start interacting with her and so, at a certain point in the discussion within a group of people he blurted out... "So Mary, you like to have fun?" She replied, "No... I hate having fun!" So you see how obvious it is that all should enjoy having fun, it is co-natural with us. Smiling is the first sign of an intellect!

Diversion is a term for fun in many other languages. It turns us away from the normal routine. Change is good and this bit of change is important because we are social. That is why people go out and interact with one another whether it be dancing, drinking, playing cards, going to the movies, concerts, working at charity events together, etc. So the first thing to having fun is realizing that it is good for you. It is an essential part of happiness because it is social, and good social life is according to our nature. God created us this way. It is also to be considered to be taking time for oneself. There is nothing wrong with taking time for oneself. People look forward to doing things they like… It also makes a person accomplish the things they need to do in order to enjoy their time of play without feeling that they should be working because after all, they don't feel like they should be working because they already got their work done. NO GUILT!

Remember, having fun is good for you!

So, have fun today! All work and no play make Jack a dull boy!

CHAPTER 19

Taking Care of the Body

a/k/a

The Case of the Sinful Sunburn

Question: Saturday night when I prayed the examen, the thought came that it was wrong of me to allow myself to get sunburned. To explain: Saturday I was pulling weeds in the front yard. It took about three hours, and it was in the heat of the day. I was listening to an audiobook, so the time went by pleasantly. I was wearing a tank top. I did notice that my back was starting to sting, but I thought, "I don't care." I really wanted to finish, and I didn't care if I got burned, so I tuned out the pain and kept going. By evening, it was a bad burn. It was my own fault, so I didn't complain.

But then when I prayed the examen that night and asked the question about what I could have done better, it seemed that my not caring about getting sunburned was sinful. I have been reflecting on that since then, and I understand that I should never do that again. But, Father, if someone confessed that to you in the Sacrament of Confession, wouldn't you think that was a weird sin to confess?

Father Jeffry: Not at all a weird sin to confess. There is a definite relationship between sunburn and cancer. We are to care for our bodies and the body of a spouse as if it were our own because it is indeed our own when married. It can also cause one to lose sleep affecting the next day or more.

CHAPTER 20

Curious about Curiosity

a/k/a

Keeping the Mind on Track

Question: I read a strange thing in *The One-Minute Aquinas*, and I wonder what you think about this: St. Thomas Aquinas considered curiosity to be a vice! In fact, he juxtaposes the "vice of curiosity" vs. "the virtue of studiousness." In more detail, it says: *"Curiosity, then, is a wrongful desire or study in pursuing knowledge that violates the temperance that moderates our desires for things. We are curious when we focus our minds on knowledge that is sinful or trivial, rather than on true wisdom, when we seek knowledge for our own pride, rather than God's glory, and when we seek knowledge of the bizarre and the lurid, rather than of the true and the beautiful...Our own age tempts us toward curiosity as never before, since a virtual universe of triviality is but a tap of a finger or a mouse click away. We'd be well advised, then, to follow the advice and the example of studious St. Thomas and focus our desires and studies on the matters that matter the most!"*

What do you think of this? This hit me between the eyes because I am one of those who taps a finger or clicks a mouse if something of interest grabs my attention when I'm online--not to sinful things--but to idle things, yes.

Father Jeffry: Curiosity for understanding that which is true is good. For that which is unnecessary, it is not. It can cause one to lose time.

Reply: Okay, Father, I will reflect on that. Actually, I'm already thinking back to last week when I didn't go to chapel because I was distracted by articles that were popping up online. I was curious and I followed my nose, but the articles really weren't anything substantial. I would have been better off to spend the hour with Jesus in the Adoration Chapel.

CHAPTER 21

Receiving Holy Communion

a/k/a

On the Tongue or In the Hand?

Question: I just skimmed an article where Cardinal Sarah is calling for the faithful to return to receiving Holy Communion on the tongue. What do you think of this? I sometimes receive on the tongue, but not usually. I could, though, if it's better to do that.

Father Jeffry: Absolutely receive on the tongue. Receiving substance or food for life is just that… receiving. When we take the Eucharist in our hand and then pick it up and feed ourselves, it becomes a distortion of what is taking place.

The Church has often depicted herself as a pelican feeding her young with her lifeblood. It is important to receive on the tongue like the baby birds, completely dependent on receiving their grace to live from the Mystical Body of Christ, rather than feeding ourselves.

CHAPTER 22

The Rosary vs. the Divine Mercy Chaplet

a/k/a

Which One to Pick?

Question: George has a question for you. Which is more powerful and important: The Rosary or the Divine Mercy Chaplet?

Father Jeffry: The Rosary or the Divine Mercy Chaplet? Both. They are not mutually exclusive. Pray them and measure the time well spent.

CHAPTER 23

What Determines My Value?

a/k/a

You Are More Than What You Do

Question: I know that my relationship with God is the most important thing, but isn't the work that I do for him the way that I show God that I love Him? It's like the Holy Spirit is saying that a relatively small amount of work is better if I am happy, than doing more work if I am not happy, which doesn't make sense to me at all! What happened to sacrifice? Like the heroic sacrifices of the saints? I want to be a saint, not a mediocre Catholic! The answer I seemed to hear seems highly suspicious to me. I am confused.

Fr. Jeffry: You are equivocating happiness with work. What is your salvation? Bringing yourself to a state of working better or a state of happiness with God? Work is not something by which we measure Christians; it is rather the fruit of a Christian in love with God. The Christian in love with God spends quality time with God and is jealous of that special time put aside for Him and for the Christian himself. That is why, even with so much work to do, Mother Teresa insisted her nuns spend much time in silent prayer. Retreat time is where you actually retreat, get away from it ALL and spend a few days getting to that point where you finally are bored out of your mind that you start really talking and listening to God. You don't know what needs to be done; God does. So, your goal in life is not to be useful; your goal is to become a Lover of God.

Reply: What you wrote has completely blown up the main drive of my life--although I did not know it to be so--which was to be useful to God because otherwise I have no value. That is how I feel tonight, Father: completely without value. The Holy Spirit has done this to me, but I don't know why. I don't know what Jesus wants from me.

Father Jeffry: Let's go over the main point again. You said, "…which was to be useful to God because otherwise I have no value." It's as if you are overriding the will of God who says to you "Kathleen, I love you for who you are, not for what you do!" And you respond that you would rather be measured according to what you do, or you will not accept that you have a value.

Consider Luke 17:10. *"So you also, when you shall have done all these things that are commanded you, say: We are unprofitable servants; we have done that which we ought to do."*

Let me make an analogy: Young men graduate from high school and go into the Marines. They all go through basic training and get torn down and then built back up, no matter whether you were the slacker or the town's favorite jock. You get built back up with some novelties, new ideas that are, at least, new to you. The most famous is that the person is a worthless POS. Wherever you came from was the worst place on earth etc. BUT then there comes the time that the sergeant tells the soldier that he is an elite lean mean fighting machine and that he belongs to the best-of- the-best warriors on the face of the earth. It is part of a necessary transformation. They did that with us in the seminary in Minnesota. They actually told us that they wanted a *tabula rasa*. They wanted us to forget all preconceived notions of Catholicism and let them reform us. That was stupid, though, because they were telling us to forget that which brought us to pursue the priesthood.

So, in Luke 17:10 it explains to us that we can't come before God and say: "Here's what I did for you..., you owe me because I am one of your best servants". Remember the workers that were all paid the same, and some got angry because they worked all day and got paid the same? Well, it seems to me that God is telling you that His love for you is more about "who" you are than what you do. It's more about you being His family rather than hired help. Remember the older brother in the Prodigal Son story? He was jealous of the love that his father showed his worthless brother upon his return. He told his father how much he had always worked and never even had a party with his friends. But the father corrected him saying that he could have had a party and that he was also owner because he was his son and that he loves him, too, precisely because he is his son. It is not what you do, it is who you are and that "who" is measured by love. Do you remember the old song? "...And they'll know we are Christians by our love, by our love; Yes, they'll know we are Christians by our love."

Be the lover in the family. That is where the doing starts.

Maybe this is just simply a purification of motives. After all, that is what Christianity is all about... not only doing the right things, but also doing them for the right reason.

Reply: I teared up as I read this. I saw myself in what you wrote about the older son yearning to be more than just an employee to his Father. I had not known how much I ached to hear Jesus say to me, "Kathleen, I love you for who you are, not for what you do!" When you wrote it, I believed it as if Jesus himself had said it. This morning in the chapel, I read in the book on learning to trust God that the destination of our journey is to trust God with our whole being, and that this is what it means to be a saint.

Just like you said: *"Your goal in life is not to be useful; your goal is to become a Lover of God."*

All right then. It is a new day, and this is my new goal.

Father Jeffry: Remember that happiness isn't the goal. The goal is living well and doing what is right. That is what makes us happy! Go for it!

CHAPTER 24

Defeating Procrastination

a/k/a

Productivity "Paula Bunyan" Style

Question: One of the many benefits of your guidance has been my growing realization that leisure time is necessary for personal development and for recreation (re-creation, as you put it). Yesterday I came to understand that one of the reasons I procrastinate is the hunger for a break from work. However, procrastination is not a healthy way or a virtuous way to take a break! When I procrastinate, I end up avoiding the work I should be doing, but I don't actually relax or recreate either. I conclude that procrastination is unloving to both self and others and a waste of the time God has given me.

I currently have 33 items listed on my to-do list, some of which have been there for several months. Example: doing our taxes. I filed a six-month extension, which comes due soon, yet I still have not started the work.

Why? Because the taxes have become so complicated ever since we bought property in Costa Rica and built the cabins there. I used to be able to do our taxes by myself, using tax prep software, but no more. Now everything has to be taken to an accountant. I resist because I don't want to do it. Inside myself, I would rather not own the property in Costa Rica than deal with all this iffy international paperwork.

The last time I confessed procrastination in confession, I admitted that it was wrong, but I didn't really do anything different about it. This time I mean to change as an act of love for God and the desire to do things His way.

Father, would it be all right with you if I report to you about this during this month? The temptation to avoid these procrastinated tasks is still very strong, despite my fervent desire to change. If I complete even one of them each day, I could be caught up in about a month. I just don't know that I will do it, if left to myself.

Father Jeffry: Yes it would be OK. Wouldn't you have an exuberant feeling once you got your taxes done? Look for a picture of an axe on the Internet. Imagine that every single item you complete is an axe chop at the tree. CHOP THE TREE DOWN!

Reply: I found a picture of a felling axe and a drawing of a barren tree. Then I added text boxes for the tasks that have been procrastinated for one reason or another. (Copy attached.) I just printed out a copy to post on the door of the classroom. This is such a great idea, Father! I am encouraged.

Sometimes I procrastinate doing a task because I am afraid I won't do it right. Sometimes I can't figure out how best to go about it. Sometimes I resent it because it seems like it should be George's job, not mine. But sometimes I just plain don't want to do it.

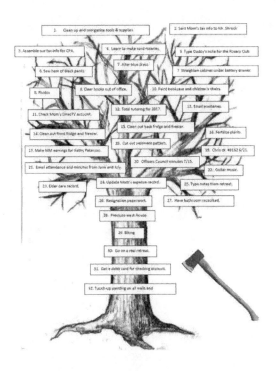

Regardless, today I've resolved to do the first task of reorganizing all my tools and gardening supplies on the back porch, even though I don't quite know how it should be done, and then I'll get rid of the rickety corner shelves on which they are currently piled. Estimated time for completion: 2 hours. I will report back on this to you tomorrow.

Thank you, Father!

Reply (*A few days later*): Good morning, Father Jeffry! I am happy to report that I finished the first project! It took me 4.5 hours to do because I had to keep stopping to take care of other duties. It took only about 2 hours of real work. I am so pleased with the result! I will attach a photo.

George was surprised when he came home from surfing and saw it! I have not told him what I am doing because I don't want any pressure from outside. This effort is for God, not anyone else.

I also did #31: Get a debit card for my checking account. I have needed to do this for almost five years, since the name of our credit union changed its name, but I never got around to it until yesterday. So, two chops on the tree today!

Last night I asked George if he would stay home from the beach today and help get our tax information assembled for the accountant. He readily agreed, saying the waves would be "mush" today. So, I will be working on #3 today, as well as #12.

Thank you so much, Father! You have turned this into an exciting game, instead of a dreaded drudgery!

Father Jeffry: Wonderful! All good news. When you have more free time when these chores are done, I want you to start benefiting from the arts like concerts, theatre, free time reading in a coffee shop for definite periods of time. I want you to do good things for yourself and enjoy them.

Reply: This is very different for me, Father, to be told to do good things for myself and to enjoy them. It has always felt selfish for me to plan fun things for myself unless those things were to be shared with someone else or were in service to others. But I am listening, Father, and I will do what you have said. I believe with all my heart that Jesus is directing me through you, which is one of the reasons why it means so much to me that you are proud of me because when you say that, it is as if you are speaking for both you and Jesus.

Father Jeffry: I am happy you are chopping down the tree and that you will clean up around the tree and keep the area clean! Again! I am proud of you.

Reply (*3 months later*): The tree is finally chopped down! George and I did the last chop together.

Father Jeffry: CONGRATULATIONS ON CHOPPING DOWN THE TREEEEEEE!!!!! WAY TO GO! I AM PROUD OF YOU!

CHAPTER 25

Going on Retreat

a/k/a

Finding Time to Be Alone with God

Question: Father Jeffry, chop #30 on the tree is to "Go on a real retreat." I have been invited to do the music for a retreat at St. Leo Abbey in Dade City, Florida. I've helped with the music on just about every retreat I've been on. Would this be okay to count as a real retreat, even though I'd be ministering, too? If it would be better for me to go on a different kind of retreat as a "real" retreat, where should I go?

Father Jeffry: No, go on a retreat with no duties. That is what a retreat is. Get away and be free completely where you eat in silence, walk, pray and go through a period where you have nothing to do so that you feel like you are wasting time. That's when you enter into yourself. I can see you dutifully preparing the music so you're really not retreating, but serving. My humble opinion.

Also, I suggest you go somewhere cold in November to experience a very different atmosphere all alone, I repeat, all alone. That's what a retreat is.

Reply: I googled "Retreats for Catholic Women" and similar searches, and I was amazed at how many retreat centers there are! Where should I go? There are so many types of retreats, too! How do I know what to pick?

Father Jeffry: You can go on the retreat but just realize that if you are working, it's just not a real retreat in my opinion. It is also important to go alone. Also, be patient because I have ordered the following book:

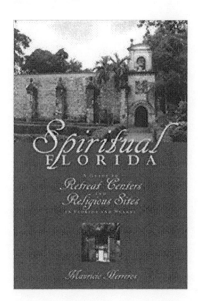

Reply: Thank you for ordering the book for me! That was so kind of you! I am looking forward to it and will be watching my mailbox.

CHAPTER 26

Temptation

a/k/a

Sin or Not?

Question: Is temptation sinful?

Father Jeffry: No, temptation in itself is not a sin… When you revel in it and allow it to play in your head for enjoyment… then the sin starts.

CHAPTER 27

Abandonment to Divine Providence

a/k/a

Giving Up…Not!

Question: What is the difference between Abandonment to Divine Providence and giving up? The former feels much like the latter to me right now.

Father Jeffry: Abandonment to Divine Providence means cooperating with God. Giving up means not trying anymore, thus, not cooperating with God.

CHAPTER 28

Worrying about Adult Children

a/k/a

How to Let Go and Let God

Question: At Mass this morning when I knelt down after receiving Jesus in Holy Communion, it seemed to me that Jesus told me He was going to cure me of worrying. In the homily, the priest had said that God would always provide for our needs. *Always.* I do believe that. I often feel inadequate to what life asks of me, though, and so I've thought that I couldn't help worrying. However, if I were having impure thoughts, I wouldn't say, "I can't help it." No, I would have to change my thoughts! God commands us not to worry, yet I've never looked at worry as something that I must change. Now I do.

Father, could I report to you about my worries as temptations against trusting God? You understand the human condition with compassion, yet you see it with a logic and clarity that I often lack. I think that, with your help, I will be able to change.

Father Jeffry: By all means report to me.

Reply: Okay, here are the worries that are keeping my stomach in a knot at the moment. Instead of trying to sublimate them, I resolved to write them down before I went to sleep last night, so that I could explain them to you. This is probably going to seem very weird, but here they are: (I listed nine worries.)

After I wrote these down in my journal, I prayed, "Jesus, I trust in You," but I realized that it wasn't completely true. I don't trust that He's going to be able to help my wayward children. That thought touched off a familiar worry that I have not done for my children what they needed, even though I tried my best. So, I will keep praying, "Jesus, I trust in You." I don't trust him completely yet as I should, but I am trying to learn to trust Him with my whole heart.

(*The next morning*): Father, Jeffry, this morning I read in the chapel from the book, *Stepping on the Serpent*, that trust takes us from our own weakness to the strength and mercy of the Father, and that the result of such complete trust is joy in the Father's care and mercy. I will meditate on this today.

Father Jeffry: Once I was working on the railroad and I said something about the Church. This guy, who was so prepotent that everybody literally called him "god" said: "Religion ain't nuthin' but a crutch for a bunch of weaklings!" I responded: "You are absolutely right! I am a weak sinner, and I need Jesus!"

Reply: Father, it appears that worries happen when I try to push away feelings of concern, rather than consciously thinking about them and praying about them. It is sometimes painful for me to "feel" the emotions and needs of other people. Just the same, it seems harmful/sinful for me to reject the part of me that is very sensitive to my own emotions and the emotions of others because it dampens the communication between God and me and because it constitutes a rejection of a gift that God has given me. Unfortunately, sensitivity to the needs and requests of others often drives me to do too much, resulting in living an unbalanced life to the detriment of my marriage, my family life, and my health and well-being. Therefore, for my own good and the good of others, my urge to help must be given boundaries.

Question (*another day*): Last week I made the decision to trust God in everything, and I believed I could do it just by choosing to do it. But the problem is that I will find my way to complete trust and be filled with faith and joy, and then something will happen to drain the joy and replace it with fear. How can I keep fear from happening and grabbing hold of me? I want to be steady. I want to stop worrying about the Church. I want to stop worrying about my adult children. Sometimes it feels as if my heart will break. Please, Father, how can my trust become unshakable?

Father Jeffry: You say, I want to be steady. You have been steady in the past. What changed? Worry. Worry is not Christian. Worry is useless. Cast it aside immediately because it is a temptation to despair. Worrying serves absolutely nothing! Trying to find a solution is one thing, but worrying about what you have no control over is not even logical.

Who made you savior? EVERYTHING doesn't depend on you.

The Church belongs to Jesus Christ Our Lord. That is why we don't carry everything; we TRUST in the LORD and give the problem to HIM. The Reality is that you CANNOT change the minds of your children nor tell them what to do once they are adults.

You have to abandon them to DIVINE PROVIDENCE. That is all you can do, that is the MAXIMUM you can do.

Reply: You hit the nail on the head. I trust Jesus with my own life, but not the lives of my children. With them, I want to see results! I have even wondered if Mother Mary understands what it's like to have children out of the Church and to be fearful for their souls. Father, even though I know that God is in control of the world, and even though I read that I should surrender, I'm not doing it! Didn't Abraham beg God to save the people of Sodom and Gomorrah? And didn't Moses beg God for mercy on the Israelites in the desert? They didn't roll over and play dead and just say, "Well, whatever you want" to God when it came to protecting the people they loved. I can't just give up or give in or surrender or abandon my babies! If I have to fight for their salvation somehow, then I will.

Father Jeffry: Wait, wait, wait… *"and even though I read that I should surrender…"* who said anything about surrender? I didn't say give up. I didn't say stop praying. We are co-operators with God. We are called to co-operate, so that, too, is our vocation. We are NOT called to WORRY. Abandoning your children to Divine Providence is an act of

TRUST which pleases Our Lord. That abandonment does not mean that you give up nor that you stop praying for them. Abraham and Moses and all the great people of the Bible who didn't give up, who bargained with God using God's own goodness, were in *active participation*, you might say, and that is not surrender, to be sure.

You quoted, "Well, whatever you want," in a rather snippy way… That translates to "Then, Thy Will be done." If there is something bad on earth, NEVER assume that God wants it that way. You hear people talk about car accidents and people dying and saying, "It was God's will!" NO! Allowing something to happen is not willing something to happen.

Reply (*after time spent in prayer*): I get it that God wants me to get on board with HIS plan, not beg Him to get on board with MY plan. He understands that sometimes His children have to go away from home in order to find their way back home, as with the prodigal son. And even though I hate it and it breaks my heart, God knows exactly where His children are. My vocation is to trust Him and pray and do what He has given me to do. Insisting that God get busy and DO something is arrogance, a product of my worry and lack of trust.

Confession at noon.

CHAPTER 29

Texting and Driving

a/k/a

Let Go (of the Phone) and Let God (Keep You Safe)!

Question: Yesterday, my hamster died. I had put her out in her exercise ball. Somehow the ball came open, and my dog caught her and killed her. I felt terrible and blamed myself for not being careful enough with her. Instead of crying and getting all upset, I remembered what St. Francis de Sales said about staying calm and bringing my soul back to the presence of God and putting everything under His will.

Last night in bed I lay there staring at my big painting of Jesus and asking Him why. This thought came: That I will feel immeasurably worse if I don't quit messing with my phone while I'm driving and someone gets hurt. I had been praying about that yesterday, asking Jesus to help me be more careful to keep the phone at bay while driving. This hard lesson ought to do it.

Father Jeffry: This is extremely serious! Do you remember when we didn't have mobile phones? The world still continued! Can you imagine having a car accident and killing people just because you wanted to answer somebody, so that they would not be offended? Can you imagine having taken the lives of several persons over nothing? And can you imagine how angry you would be if someone was texting and killed a family member of yours? I say that just to put it into perspective. I do not use my phone when I drive, and I ask people who are driving not to use their phone either. Some people just don't touch their phone until they pull over, not even to see who called or sent a message.

Reply (*sometime after promising to refrain from distracted driving*): I need to tell you that I broke my promise about not using the phone while driving when I drove between DeLand and Tampa and back. I had the phone out to use as a GPS, and the temptation to pick it up when it was a family member contacting me did me in. Repeatedly. One of the times it could have easily caused a wreck. I know it is wrong to be willing to take risks with my own life and the lives of others. I am sorry for it, but I don't think I will be able to resist the temptation, if the phone is up for me to use as a GPS. I'm sorry, Father, to God and to you.

Father Jeffry: Could you imagine living with having caused an accident that killed someone, whether old or young? Can you imagine your feelings toward anyone who killed your grandchildren in a car wreck because they were on the phone? The problem is that all the people that had accidents while on the phone thought that they wouldn't have an accident... BUT they did.

Reply (*later*): My pastor heard my confession today about the distracted driving, and I confessed that this was the fourth time confessing this sin. I told him I downloaded an app that was supposed to give an automated message that I'm driving and using the GPS, but when I tested it yesterday, it didn't work. So, now I didn't know what to do. I said that maybe I just can't use the phone as a GPS. He paused, and then he said, "No, I want you to pray to overcome this temptation."

He talked a lot about Mother Mary and how she received so many graces, having the second greatest mission next to Jesus, but she lived out her vocation in silence, and he wants me to embrace that silence. I'm not exactly sure what that means in practice, but I will pray about it.

For penance, he gave me only one Hail Mary, but he said to pray it as a consecration to Mary.

CHAPTER 30

A Sense of Mission

a/k/a

What Is My Role in God's Plan?

Question: I watch you and George do great things for the glory of God and the salvation of souls, and yet it seems that when I try to do likewise, I am called to do small things instead. It seems that my work is small and hidden, revolving around George and my mother and my children and grandchildren and the paperwork and phone calling of parish ministries and praying for you and your ministry, instead of moving out into the world to evangelize, as you and George do. I do get to serve one-on-one by taking Holy Communion to the nursing home residents once a month, and I love serving at the altar and filling in for music at the Masses when needed. For the most part, I am content in this life and grateful.

Yet, there is always this nagging feeling of inadequacy, of being less than I should be or could be. I don't know how to put it into words, except to compare it to the angst of an actor who aims to be a star, but instead ends up playing supporting roles. I know that Mother Mary's life was mostly this way, too, revolving around her family and hidden away. In my mind I know that whatever God asks of me is what I should be doing with my life. And yet, that "head knowledge" does not get through to my heart. I compare myself to you and George and find myself wanting.

Is it really enough to play a supportive role, rather than being on the front lines of evangelization? Or is there something more I should be doing? Is this a lack of humility or a lack of courage?

Father Jeffry: You should never compare yourself to anybody. Of course it is impossible not to do it to a certain extent, but all considerations must be in accordance with your vocation. Your vocation is that of a married woman and the testimony that you give.

If you are living your vocation to marriage, it is not a supporting role! You are starring in a role that you were chosen for by God. Humility is always necessary by all at all times. You are more courageous than most because you examine yourself.

CHAPTER 31

Spiritual Fatherhood and Motherhood

a/k/a

Spiritual Daughterhood and Sonship

Question: For some reason, this morning I felt called to meditate on the difference between spiritual fatherhood and spiritual motherhood. You are spiritual father to me, and I, your spiritual daughter. But at the same time, last August I officially adopted you on the <u>Foundation of Prayer for Priests</u> as my priest to spiritually "mother". And so I pray for you and seek to support you and your vocation and your mission in any way that I can.

I revisited the website this morning. I was struck by the difference between spiritual fatherhood and motherhood as presented there, seeing parallels to biological fatherhood and motherhood in the lay realm: **"The priest is 'another Christ,' a bridegroom of the Church, and demonstrates his spiritual fatherhood through his service to the people of God as spiritual head and shepherd. The** ordained priesthood is the only vocation by which the man is sacramentally marked with an indelible sign that enables him to participate in the priesthood of Jesus Christ, the Eternal High Priest. The priest is anointed and empowered to be a real spiritual father in nourishing and forming spiritual children, who are called to become saints. The priest begets spiritual children in the way that Jesus did—by evangelizing the faithful (preaching and teaching), by offering sacrifices on their behalf (the Holy Mass), and by laying down his life (dying to self in the service of others) so that his spiritual children may return safely to the Father's house.

"Spiritual mothers transmit spiritual life to priests through their communion with Jesus, the Eternal High Priest, and Mary, Mother of Priests. It is through the sacramental rivers of grace that a woman, as a daughter of the Church, receives her spiritual life. In turn, she, as a spiritual mother, becomes a vessel of life-giving grace. A spiritual mother encounters the Eternal High Priest in the Eucharist and then, like Mary, carries Christ to others, offering prayers and sacrifices along the way. To priests, she mirrors Mary. The vocation to spiritual motherhood of priests is at the heart of the New Evangelization, since by the intercession of spiritual mothers, graces are obtained to renew priests and strengthen them in spreading the Gospel."

Afterward, I picked up Kathleen Beckman's book, *Praying for Priests*, off my bookshelf, and I will look through it to see if there seems to be something in particular that I should pray for you today.

Thank you, Father, for everything you have done for me. I

am so very grateful for you.

Father Jeffry: Did I tell you that today is the 10th anniversary of my ordination?

Reply: Congratulations, Father Jeffry!!!! You didn't tell me, but I guess the Holy Spirit wanted me to know.

CHAPTER 32

Freedom and Authority

a/k/a

Faithfulness

Question: I woke up with a gnawing question. In the final judgment, Jesus said we would be judged on works of mercy. "I was hungry, and you gave me food. I was thirsty, and you gave me drink...". He never said we would be judged on how humbly we obeyed authority. It just seems that if obedience to human authority was so all-fired important, He would have mentioned it in the final judgment. Just saying.

While I know there are plenty of Scriptures that state human authority comes from God, in life it also seems that progress is often made by those who think outside the box and shake off the restrictions placed on them by an authority that cares more about power than progress. Authority exercised with love and understanding seems to result in an obedient heart, but authority that seeks to dominate and demean seems to result in rebellion. But then, of course, I am speaking of the subject's perception of the mindset of the one in authority. When Eve disobeyed God, she perceived that He was holding back and being dishonest with her because the serpent had planted that idea in her mind. She was wrong.

Father, I do not understand why I am content and even eager to obey you, while the idea of obeying anyone else, including George, makes me feel cornered and restricted and fearful. I cannot seem to come to terms with this. My head, my heart, and my will won't line up.

You told me once to "obey the love between us" with George. I can do that, but I am reluctant to obey *him*. Is obeying the love between us enough?

Father Jeffry: I see that you see an obedient relationship as one similar to master and slave. Remember that you are co-equals in a relationship. You will also have to meditate on what obedience means and why God desires that the man, as head of the family, should have a certain authority.

Reply: In Father Cedric's book, he is currently talking about freedom and how central the desire for freedom is. He says we are responsible for our own freedom, and that rather than being dominated by impulses and feelings, we are led by God's Holy Spirit into the fullness of freedom. He says that either we serve sin or we serve God, but we can't serve both at the same time. I get that. I guess that is why Jesus is so insistent that every part of my life be under His authority and grace, no exceptions.

Living under authority is not as hard as I thought it would be. I am very surprised at how secure and protected and free that it makes me feel. Even regarding sleep, it feels good

that the matter is settled. I know what I'm supposed to do--
what God expects of me and what I've promised you.

CHAPTER 33

Cosmetic and Reconstructive Surgery

a/k/a

Is the Pursuit of Beauty Vain or Virtuous?

Question: I just finished reading a book by Shaunti Feldhahn, entitled *For Women Only: what you need to know about the inner lives of men.* The author did tons of research with men and shared the results. The aim of the book is to encourage understanding and support of the husband in the way he needs to be loved.

Basically, the book said that men are visual and that the man takes it personally how his woman looks, as if her looks determine how he feels he is perceived by others. The book says it like, if the wife is beautiful and happy, he is a great guy. If she is frumpy and unhappy, he is a loser. That seems incredibly shallow to me, but the author says it's simply how men are wired. So, if I want to make my man feel loved, then I have to care as much about my outside beauty as my inward beauty.

Looks like that cost money! If men care so much about what their wives looks like, maybe I should spend the money to get the spider veins from multiple pregnancies removed from my legs, so I'll be more comfortable at the beach.

This all seems so opposite of what Scripture says, but what do I know? Men say women are hard to understand, but men are hard for women to understand, too. I'm going to regret having sent you this, I know it. But I'm sending it.

Father Jeffry: No problem! Good to spill the beans. I didn't know that there was a procedure for the spider veins. From the Catholic point of view, one can have an operation on the body to do something positive and not negative. For example, you can remove a part of the body that is detrimental, but you cannot remove a part of the body which is good and is causing no harm. The maximum is that you can do what your body would do if it could. The body would never have a vasectomy, for example, but it would heal a defect in the body, such as a hernia or the vein problem. Do what is good for you and your marriage.

Reply: I thought the desire to be beautiful was morally wrong. I mean, we women are set before us examples like St. Rose of Lima, who rubbed pepper in her face so that others would not compliment her for her beauty. And in the Bible, women are constantly warned against vanity and told to concentrate on inner beauty as the only beauty that matters. That's confusing because husbands think just the opposite: that outer beauty is just as important as inner beauty. But I asked Jesus last night, "Is this for real? Is it *really* okay for me to want to be beautiful for George and to do what it takes to be so?" What I got back from Jesus--not in words--was that He is directing me through you, and I should continue to trust your guidance.

I have never been one to care about fashion. I opt for comfort. I wear the same dresses for many years, and I wear shoes until they literally fall apart. My hairstyle is simple and easy.

I reviewed what St. Francis de Sales had to say about how to dress: "For my own part I should like my devout man or woman to be the best dressed person in the company, but the least fine or splendid, and adorned, as Saint Peter says, with 'the imperishable jewel of a gentle and quiet spirit.' (1 Pt 3:4)." In Pope Francis' list of New Year's Resolutions, he says, "Choose the more humble purchase."

Honestly, I don't know what the right thing is to do here. George encourages me to shop for new things, but I rarely do. Should I please my husband by being more stylish?

Father Jeffry: YES.

CHAPTER 34

Keeping Secrets

a/k/a

Keeping the Mystery Alive

Question: I am intrigued by what you said about how spouses should never really know everything about the other because then the mystery is gone. What do you mean? A priest I know used to say, "You're only as sick as your secrets," which I took to mean that spouses shouldn't keep secrets or their marriage will suffer. You must mean something different. I do keep some things to myself, but it would be nice to be able to do that without feeling guilty about it. I wonder how you know so much about marriage when you're a priest, but I have never gone wrong doing what you told me to do concerning George, even when it was hard.

I am very interested to learn more about what you meant by not losing the mystery. What mystery? And how does it work? How is it good for a husband not to know everything about his wife?

Father Jeffry: Have you ever been fascinated by something you understand completely? No. Fascination deals with an element of the unknown. Did you ever say to a person, "I didn't know that about you?" And it was always in relation to a pleasant surprise. Remember that we are still individuals and not even in the Bible does it say that you must know your spouse totally. There is a difference between keeping secrets from your spouse and your spouse knowing absolutely everything about you.

CHAPTER 35

Time Alone

a/k/a

What to Do When Your Husband Is Traveling

Question: This morning I want to ask your guidance about something. As I told you yesterday, George will be leaving for Costa Rica for 10 days this coming Monday. He told me last night that he would miss me while he is gone. I replied in a lighthearted, teasing tone, "And yet you will still leave me." He pulled me close and said something that I don't remember. Then he added that he was going to talk to his property manager about listing the cabins for sale. He added, "If God wills us to sell the cabins, then a buyer will come forward. If He wants us to keep them, then one won't." I'm fine with that.

I don't really understand how husbands are about traveling. I mean, I don't understand how a man leaves his wife to surf with his buddies, but thinks she's going to believe him when he says he's going to miss her. If he misses me, it must not be very much. I have told him before how much I miss him when he's gone, but it doesn't change anything.

This time I intend to try _not_ to miss him. I am determined to look at these 10 days as time for me to do things that I can't do while he's home. When he leaves, I am always left to figure out how I will handle things here at home on my own, which I will do. I don't need him to take care of me. I can take care of myself. It's a good thing to be independent in an uncertain world.

But, Father, the strange thing is that he seems to hope that I will be happy while he's gone, but at the same he hopes I will miss him. That seems unfair to me and illogical, too! And when he comes home, everything is supposed to go back to the way it was before he left. But his leaving requires me to become more independent, so I don't feel the same when he comes back. I feel distant and self-protective, and then I have to work at overcoming those feelings. Apparently, wives do not operate the way husbands do.

I would not bring this up with you except that you have told me more than once that George is my vocation, and I know you are right, but being a good wife to him is a struggle for me sometimes. He and I are alike on many things, but so different in others. However, the deal that George and I made when we married was "I don't control you, you don't control me." So, if he wants to go surfing in his Costa Rica with his buddies, I shouldn't get in the way or feel resentful or sad or whatever. If I can get myself to look at this time apart from George as God's will for me, then maybe I will feel better about it.

(Later that day) Today when I left the church, the story about the prodigal son came to my mind--the part about the brother who was envious and resentful of the son who came home. The thought came that the reason the brother was envious was because he no longer knew where he stood with his Father. He thought maybe the Father loved the son who had returned more than him. Then the thought came to me that this is my story, too, because I keep wondering whether Jesus loves George more than me because He treats him so differently from the way He treats me.

I teared up, but a parking lot is not a good place to cry. I couldn't go to the Adoration Chapel because it's closed for renovations. So, I pushed away the tears and drove home. I have been thinking today, though, about what the Father said to the older son. He didn't say, "I love you," but He did say, "You are always with me and everything I have is yours." Maybe that's how God says, "I love you" to people, by being with them and sharing everything with them, instead of saying it in words. I have been thinking, too, about how there are such varied personalities among the saints, and yet God still loves all of the saints so much that He has taken them to heaven to be with Him. I want so much to be a saint and be with Jesus forever!

When George goes to heaven, he wants to hear Jesus say, "Well done, good and faithful servant!" When I go to heaven, I long for Jesus to hug me close in His arms, just like you hugged me when you came to visit us last week. George and I are alike in some ways, but we are so different in other ways. I guess that's why God doesn't treat us the same-- because we're *not* the same.

Father Jeffry: You said: *"So, I pushed away the tears. I have been* *thinking today, though, about what the Father said to him. He didn't say, 'I love you,' but He did say, 'You are always with me and everything I have is yours.' Maybe that's how God says, 'I love you' to people—by being with them and sharing everything with them, instead of saying it in words.* If you remember how I pressed on for a correct understanding of words, well, here is something to think about. "Being." We talked about this word when I was there. Again you said: "…By being with them and sharing everything with them." That is it! You get it. By being with them! Because this is a way of informing: Giving information and love. We are held in existence by God. It is a continual act! He is always holding us in being. Eventually you might say that we would run out of finite things to know and contemplate and that is true; that is why God, in His infinity will always teach us new Truths. These Truths are none other than Himself, his BEING, that which is *"ad intra"* as opposed to *"ad extra"*, that which is outside of God!

Also, remember this: Time alone is time to grow one's self. Enjoy your time to do the things that you like to do.

Reply: Father Jeffry, I love the way you explain things! When I read what you wrote about God *being* with us, it all made complete sense to me, connecting what you had taught me when you were here with what it seems God is trying to teach me now. While I prayed Morning Prayer this morning, I kept thinking about God being with me every moment and how He is always loving us and helping us to grow, and I felt lightness and joy in my heart!

I will remember what you said about happiness being the choice to dwell on positive thoughts based on God's infinite love for me, and I have determined to begin putting it into practice right away.

I have also embraced what you said about time alone being time to grow and do the things I like to do. I don't feel resentful anymore. I am actually looking forward to it! I will get to read more. I will also watch more videos from the New St. Thomas Institute, which I have not done for a while. I will crochet on the baby blanket for our new grandson who is due in July, and I will do some sewing and gardening and working out.

While I miss cooking for George when he's gone, a drawback of cooking for him is that I end up eating a lot of foods that are good for his blood type (AB), but not for mine (O+). So, while he is gone, I will make a game of eating ONLY type O recommended foods. It should be interesting to see how my body reacts. I have gained a good 10 pounds in recent years, and I would like to return to my ideal weight. Supposedly, eating only foods that are beneficial for one's own blood type helps the body naturally maintain the right weight. We'll see. I will try not to doubt George's love. And I will offer up not getting to go to Costa Rica for the intentions of Jesus and Mary.

Father Jeffry: Good decision after a long bout of stubbornness! Hahaha. Be glad you're normal!

Reply *(the next morning)*: Hey, Father Jeffry! George brought me roses last night, which led to a romantic evening. I guess he is going to miss me after all!

◆ ◆ ◆

CHAPTER 36

Purifying the Vessels

a/k/a

The Wisdom

Question: I saw the article you posted on Facebook about the correct prayer position for the laity when praying the Our Father during Mass. I have read that before, too, but I didn't pay much attention to it until you posted it. Everyone in our church prays with uplifted hands or holding hands during the Our Father. It will be easy for me to stop doing that when I am altar serving, but what about when I am sitting with the congregation? Do I just ignore the people beside me when they hold out their hands to join? It's not easy to correct a wrong practice when everyone is doing it. It almost seems like those instructions would need to come from the pastor to effect the change.

Father Jeffry: If you fold your hands and close your eyes and stay that way even if someone taps you on the shoulder, then you can continue praying that way. I hate holding hands during the Our Father! Especially during flu season. I will eliminate the sign of peace during flu season and tell people that.

Reply: Yesterday I served Mass for a retired priest who lives in our area. Before Mass, he told the sacristan and me that he always says the Mass in Latin when he's at home on his own. He used to teach Latin, he told us, and he concentrates better when praying in Latin rather than English.

I have to be on alert during Mass because he does things differently from the other priests. He purifies the vessels on the altar, as I saw you do in Costa Rica, rather than at the credence table.

Father Jeffry: It is not logical to purify the vessels on the credence table because one is (illogically) purifying a chalice from containing THE PUREST BEING IN THE UNIVERSE. ONE WOULD DO WELL TO SAY, "The Ablutions". This is why the Mass from before and DURING the VATICAN Council II IS MORE LOGICAL:

1. A flood of Extraordinary Ministers of the Holy Eucharist causes confusion and makes it impossible to PROPERLY clean the chalices on the CORPORAL as is necessary to show respect for Our Lord.

2. As was the norm in the past no one but no one touched a chalice but the priest. He put it away after Mass and he got it out before Mass as part of his ritual.

Your priest probably does the ablutions with wine first as it is more noble than water to be mixed with the Blood of Christ.

Reply: You are right that he does the ablutions with wine first, which is different from what the other priests and deacons do. I wondered why he did that, but I learned a long time ago to bring both cruets to him after Communion. I am glad to know why.

I think you are right, too, Father, that it was better when only the priest touched the chalice. I think that with so many Extraordinary Ministers, we have become too casual about the Holy Eucharist, not fully appreciating the awesome presence of Jesus. It is one of the things I liked about the Latin Mass in Sanford, that everyone received Holy Communion on the tongue from the priest.

Ever since you explained about praying the Our Father with eyes closed and hands folded, I have done that. George and Mom, too.

CHAPTER 37

Not Doing Enough

a/k/a

Being Too Busy

Question: I long to spend more time with George, to relax and have fun, to have time to stay caught up with my home and available to my family, but I don't know how to get rid of the inner fear of falling short, of not being enough, of not doing enough. I am praying to Jesus and Mother Mary for help.

Father Jeffry: Take it easy and don't worry about not filling up every moment with work. Blame it on me because it is my desire that you not take on any more work but that you take time absolutely for fun and to spend time with George at the beach. Again I repeat this is your vocation; you make each other happy by giving yourself to each other. That's the most important thing you can do in your life! Again, that is the most important thing you can do in your life!

CHAPTER 38

Paperwork Purgatory

a/k/a

Joy and Patience

Question: I am working on paperwork. They say love makes the world go 'round, but paperwork seems to be the glue that holds together much of ministry and business. At least, that is my experience.

(*Later...*) I am still doing what seems to be endless paperwork between caring for my Mom and tutoring students, trying to get caught up.

(*Still later...*) I feel like I am in limbo...or rather, stuck in paperwork purgatory...waiting for salvation. I know I am being melodramatic, but it is the way of things.

Father Jeffry: Unfortunately, there are exterior obligations imposed upon us. Do them with joy and patience. This is your reality.

Reply: Yes, Father. Joy and patience. I'm going to write that on a sticky note and tack it to my computer screen.

CHAPTER 39

Health vs. Work

a/k/a

Vocation as the Prime Factor

Question: Last week when I went for my checkup with my doctor, he said I need more exercise. So, I know that, but there are other priorities. George had come with me, and he agreed with the doctor. According to them, caring for my health takes priority over work and ministry.

I would not have concluded that.

I am praying to reorder my priorities according to God's and Mother Mary's will for me, but it is unsettling. I can't get any sense of rhythm and organization at all. You had said it was all about becoming my own master, which meant becoming a good disciple. But I don't feel like I am becoming my own master at all. Instead, I feel like all control is being taken away.

Father Jeffry: We can't always be rigid with our schedule. If we are, others will see us as proud of our ability to stay on schedule yet make victims of others, victims in so far that they are denied our love and attention.

George is right! Your health comes first. If not, then everyone will be taking care of you! If your husband, who is there for your best interest, notices that you are tired and need to stop working and rest, then that is when you should obey the love between you, which is manifest in his concern for your well-being. Can you imagine having a husband that said, "I know you're tired, but you still have the rest of the kitchen to clean before you come to bed." Which is better, the first or the latter?

Reply: I have thought about your email all day. I can absolutely imagine being told that no matter how tired you are, you need to get the work done. That is how I was raised, and that is how I have lived my life. To put one's own needs first was taught to me as being selfish and self-centered. The needs of others were always to come first.

I was surprised that you said straight out that my health comes first before work and ministry. That changes things.

I understand what you said about not being rigid, but I get criticized for the opposite so much! Sure, people will say to me, "You need to learn how to say no." Lately, though, I have countered with, "So, the next time *you* ask me for something, I should say 'no' then, right?" At which point, they chuckle and have no reply.

Father Jeffry: You said, *"You are very sure about this—that my health comes first before the welfare of others?"* In the context of vocation, i.e., what one is called to by God, our vocation is a "giving of self" and this gift of self must be a worthy gift, not a poor, ill-suited gift. That reasoning is that your vocation is first and foremost measured in your relationship to George and how you offer yourself to him and he to you, of course. You offer your life, i.e., your years. Can you logically conclude that you can live in such a way as to risk your life, heart attack, nerve problems, stress (which is physically debilitating) and by doing anything else that is detrimental to health? Not with impunity. No, one must seriously see their duty to God and man within the context of their vocation.

Who am I? You are a child of God created to know, love and serve Him and this, by God's will, is to be done in full cooperation with your husband, George. We will offer ourselves one to another in order to edify the domestic church according to 1 Corinthians 12:7 "Now to each one the manifestation of the Spirit is given for the common good." This edification cannot benefit from the absence of a person; this is why we love life and want to continue living even when faced with our faith which professes a loving God who wants us to be in His Divine Presence.

Reply: Father, this will be a major change for me, almost as much as when you told me that I needed to anchor my life on prayer. I have never lived marriage this way. I don't think George has either. But I finally get what you meant when you told me that George is my vocation. I mean, I understood that in being married to him that I am called to be faithful to him and helpful and loving. But I never understood that my vocation is measured by *how* I offer myself to him. I have never considered that my stress and health affect the gift of myself to him. I have not even put his needs before those of other people. Not really.

From what you said, everything I do must be weighed against how my actions and choices affect George. It makes sense. It's just a big change from "I don't control you; you don't control me", which is how we set up our relationship to start with. We aren't so cautious anymore, though, about one being controlled by the other.

Father Jeffry: In a good way, you will be measured by your mutual complicity in your project of life. You are co-creators of your relationship. In a similar way, you learn from this relationship in order to be co-creators of your relationship with God. Why is all this so important? Because love is the result! Between you two and between you two and God.

Reply (*the next day*): Last night I told George that I had taken his advice and had written you about not being able to say "no" to people and that you had addressed the problem in the context of vocation. I related to George that you said he is my vocation and that putting my health at risk affects my gift of self to him. And then I told him that I realized I haven't really been putting his needs above the needs of others and that I have allowed a lot of time stress and emotional stress to affect our relationship by not putting a limit on the number of students I take on.

Well, that opened the door to a very fruitful discussion! I asked him what would be different if he could change things--what would make our relationship better in his eyes. He told me he missed the carefree, relaxed time we used to have. "Me, too," I said. We do lots of things together, but they're usually work or ministry, not relaxing or enjoying free time. Then he asked me the same thing. I told him that I wanted to be able to have time to go to the gym and work out, so that I wouldn't have this constant underlying feeling of jealousy towards his going surfing at the beach every day. He thought it was a good idea!

I feel positively motivated to make the change now, instead of dreading it, because I understand how the time drain and my added stress affect George personally, as well as damaging my gift of self to him. The joy of our discussion led to a very joyful, intimate encounter before going to sleep. You were so right that our "mutual complicity in the project of life" does indeed lead to love between George and me--and between us and God!

I can't thank you enough, Father Jeffry! I would never have guessed that the solution to my difficulty in saying "no" to people would lie in living my vocation this way and in being mindful of how I give myself to George.

CHAPTER 40

What to Do with Temptations

a/k/a

Is It Good to Confess Them or Not?

Question: You remember that Mother Mary told me that I should tell you about temptations, or so it seemed to me. I know you said I should be careful about assigning messages as coming from her, and I am trying to be just that. In fact, I argued about this today with her. First, I said to her that people don't even confess temptations in the Sacrament of Reconciliation. And then, I asked her for a sign that she really meant for me to do that, and that it wasn't just my imagination. Well, at the start of nap time, I was reading *True Devotion to Mary*, and then, when I got up, I looked online to see if temptations are to be confessed, and immediately came upon this article:
https://rcspirituality.org/ask-priest-often-can-go-confession/.

I understand from this that revealing temptations to you is

probably a good thing, but to me, it is harder than revealing sins. I guess that's because I have a lot more temptations than I have sins, or at least I think that is the way of it.

I am stalling. So, out with it. Last night and today I have been bothered by a temptation to impure thoughts, which hasn't happened to me in a long time. I don't know why it happened now, but I don't want it, and I didn't consent to it. In fact, I grabbed the holy water bottle last night and blessed myself to make it go away. Today I was at Mass when it happened, and I just kept saying the name of Jesus and it went away pretty fast.

Father Jeffry: Rejoice! You are on the right track. Temptations come from a person and that person wants you to be in a state of guilt before God. So, that person gives you the temptations at a most inappropriate time so that your soul feels as if your soul was intentionally creating the temptations. Don't be fooled. Saints have suffered many temptations in this manner. Laugh in the devil's face and say: "The Lord is my Shepherd!"

CHAPTER 41

Starting the Day

a/k/a

Let's Go!

Question: Good morning, Father Jeffry! After such a peaceful, easy-going day yesterday, I woke up this morning with an unsettled, uncomfortable feeling. I imagine it results from unremembered dreams--I know I had a series of them, but I don't remember them. And I assume that the dreams reflected the unfinished business of yesterday, as much of my to-do list did not get done.

Father Jeffry: Every day should start like you come out of confession... starting anew! You cannot relive yesterday but only live today well. Thank God for this day and say... Let's go! Have a good one!

CHAPTER 42

The Mature Response to God

a/k/a

Does Breaking a "Rule" = Sin?

Question: While I know that lying is always hurtful, I am not convinced that disobedience is always wrong or always hurtful. It seems to me that obedience is sort of a fluid situation. Sometimes it's right to follow directions, but sometimes it's better not to. It all depends on the situation. Even Jesus did that. Like when He and His apostles ate the heads of grain while they were walking along, and somebody said, "You guys are disobeying the rules," and He basically said, "The situation calls for it." And when people objected that He was breaking the rules by healing on the Sabbath, He basically said again, "The situation calls for it." If He could set rules aside when the situation called for it, then it seems to me that I, as His follower, ought to be able to do that, too.

If I am wrong about this, please tell me how and why. I am

praying about this and struggling with it inside.

Father Jeffry: I told you long ago that I do not exact obedience *from* you. I expect practicalities motivated by love of God and family.

Question (*at a later date*): Okay, I understand that you don't expect from me obedience to "rules" as arbitrary orders--you never did--but to be motivated by love of God and love of family. I believe that is what Jesus wants of me, too! So, whatever I do now will be based on love of God, love of family, and love of others. *Every action based on love.* Only where I fall short of that will I consider my thoughts and actions be sin.

Father Jeffry: I am happy that you arrived at this conclusion. It is a mature response. Responsibility is just that... how we respond to the movements of the Holy Spirit in our hearts.

CHAPTER 43

The Obedience of Christ

a/k/a

How Could Jesus Learn Obedience?

Question: Father Jeffry, I don't understand this part of today's second reading, and I never have. What does this mean?

"Son though he was, he learned obedience from what he suffered; and when he was made perfect, he became the source of eternal salvation for all who obey him." (Hebrews 5:8-9)

Father Jeffry: *For as by the disobedience of one man, many were made sinners; so also by the obedience of one, many shall be made just.* (Romans 5:19 Douay-Rheims 1899 American Edition) (DRA) *He humbled himself, becoming obedient unto death, even to the death of the cross.* (Philippians 2:8 Douay-Rheims 1899 American Edition) (DRA)

Christ was on a mission. He was the anointed one… that is what "Christ" means. As we should work out our salvation with fear and trembling, so too, the Christ effectuated our salvation in fear and trembling. Remember how he sweat blood in the Garden of Olives? He knew the suffering that he was going to undertake.

CHAPTER 44

The Origin of the Soul

a/k/a

Where Did I Come From?

Question: Regarding the afterlife, I have one last question that has come up before; it re-surfaced when I listened to the audiobook, *To Heaven and Back*, by Father John Michael Tourangeau. Simply put, where does the soul come from? When a baby is a one-celled zygote, does he or she have a soul? If the soul is spiritual, then it can't be generated by the cells or even by the energy put out by the cells. So, how does the baby get a soul?

Father Jeffry: Most excellent question! Most excellent observation that a spiritual soul cannot be generated by the cells or by the energy put out by the cells. Let's look at it systematically...

Is there an operation in the zygote? Is it growing and growing by its own principle of life, or is it being informed by the principle of life of its mother? It is growing on its own. Does one receive several souls, or is there only one soul in a being? I would posit that there is only one for obvious reasons. Therefore, since the creation of a human being is due to the sexual relationship between a man and a woman, their union bringing into being a child or more, and that union due to the strictly natural bringing into being of an animal, that intellectual soul is not automatically concluded from the union. The intellectual soul would need a cause able to create it. And here is where God comes in... GOD INFUSES THE SOUL INTO MAN. Man, woman, and God are all three co-creators with God! What a dignity!

CHAPTER 45

Facing the Public

a/k/a

Is It Okay to Hide My Feelings?

Question: Father Jeffry, you are always so upbeat in your Facebook posts, yet one time when I commented to you that you seemed always to be happy, you said, "Actually, I'm quite angry right now." You didn't look it, not a bit. Is it that you simply make up your mind to be pleasant to others, no matter what is going on inside of you?

Father Jeffry: Well, one can be angry without losing control or letting it control you. And, although angry, I would not show you my anger.

Reply: I guess my question is: Is it dishonest to present one face to others, while feeling completely different on the inside? You would say it's okay to keep my emotions to myself, right?

Father Jeffry: Sure. You don't owe anything to people, i.e., to let them know how you feel, if it is not their business.

CHAPTER 46

Wasting Time

a/k/a

YouTube vs. You Work

Question: This morning when it was time to get to work, I checked my phone for messages, but then I saw notifications from YouTube. And well, I started scrolling through those. Before I knew it, I was off task with technology. Father, I know better than to be playing on my phone when I am supposed to be working.

Father Jeffry: These things on YouTube are amusing. But, on reflection 99% useless. One has to say to oneself: "My time will be better spent, and I will be happier, doing something important."

CHAPTER 47

Holy Communion

a/k/a

How Long, O Lord?

Question: I seem to remember that St. Faustina said her Holy Communion lasted from one Communion to the next, not the 15 minutes that I have read in other places. What do you think about that, Father?

Father Jeffry: That is the reality that Christ dwells within us. Communion is both a sign and a sacrament which effects what it signifies. The reality is that the Father and the Holy Spirit are both spirits. They do not have a body. Jesus does, and it is glorified. All three persons have the Divine Life or the Divine Nature and are not restricted by time and space. They are where they 'act' and so if they influence your spirit, which operates within your body, because it animates your body, then the Divine Life is present to you. You receive the Body, Blood, Soul, and Divinity of Jesus in Holy Communion. He is present and communicating with you, informing you and forming you.

CHAPTER 48

The Latin Mass

a/k/a

Facing Ad Orientem

Question: What is the big deal about the priest celebrating part of the Latin Mass with his back to the people? Jesus didn't do that. So, why do some conservatives think we should go back to that? I like being able to see what the priest is doing. It makes it easier to participate.

Father Jeffry: The matter of the priest having his back to the people is comparable to a bus driver. No one would say that he is turning his back to the people but rather that he is doing what he should be doing, looking at the road. The same goes for the priest…

"Te igniter, clementissime Pater, per Iesum Christum, Filium tuum, Dominum nostrum, supplices rogamus ac petimus,"

"We come to you, Father, with praise and thanksgiving, through Jesus Christ your Son."

At this point, after the readings that were directed to the congregation, the priest, *in persona Christi*, turns to His Father and speaks to His Father, towards the East where altars have for centuries been oriented towards the East from where the sun rises. From there we await Jesus Christ, the Light of the World to show Himself. That is why a priest should put a crucifix on the altar in order to face Jesus Christ crucified because the priest is offering Himself, as Jesus Christ CRUCIFIED to His Father at least liturgically EAST.

The dialogue is between the priest and God the Father. In years past the Roman Canon I, which is the first Eucharistic prayer, was spoken in an inaudible voice; only the server should be able to hear him. This is a modern-day invention that we have to see and hear everything that happens. The Orthodox priests go through doors behind the iconostasis and do the consecration completely out of sight from the congregation. There is a mystery happening and yet even seeing it happen, one cannot grasp it any better; rather, I would say that it is even detrimental to the comprehension of the mystery because one takes for granted what is happening and reduces it to almost magical words and breaking bread. We can't understand how it happens, but our Faith tells us it does!

If I had to choose between the old Mass and the new Mass for the rest of my life, I would definitely choose the old Mass because it is holier in every aspect in my humble opinion. Latin is holier and MUCH MORE SACRED!

Check these out these articles:

http://www.newliturgicalmovement.org/2016/02/the-

devil-hates-latin-says-exorcist.html#.XU37FS2ZPVs
https://unamsanctamcatholicam.blogspot.com/2008/01/d
oes-devil-hate-latin.html

Question: When you advocate the Mass in Latin, do you
mean doing it the way EWTN does it, with the Gloria and
Sanctus, etc., sung in Latin, but with the readings and homily
in English? What other parts would be in Latin?

Father Jeffry: There are two forms of the Roman Mass, the
Ordinary Form and the Extraordinary Form. The
Extraordinary form is the Mass that was used before and
during the Second Vatican Council. The Ordinary form is
the Mass which is said all over the world now.

Unfortunately, many bishops have taken a hard stance
against the Extraordinary Form of the Mass, accusing those
who follow the Extraordinary Form of causing
division. These bishops go so far as to be disobedient to
universal law (*Summorum Pontificum* as of July 7, 2007) by
absolutely prohibiting priests from saying the Mass in the
Extraordinary form. It is explicitly stated in law thus: *"Art.
2. In Masses celebrated without a congregation, any Catholic priest of
the Latin rite, whether secular or regular, may use either the Roman
Missal published in 1962 by Blessed Pope John XXIII or the Roman
Missal promulgated in 1970 by Pope Paul VI, and may do so on any
day, with the exception of the Easter Triduum. For such a celebration
with either Missal, the priest needs no permission from the Apostolic
See or from his own Ordinary."*

Here is the link so you can read the original document:
https://w2.vatican.va/content/benedict-
xvi/en/motu_proprio/documents/hf_ben-xvi_motu-
proprio_20070707_summorum-pontificum.html.

Also read the letter from the Pope which accompanied *Motu Proprio*:
http://w2.vatican.va/content/benedict-xvi/en/letters/2007/documents/hf_ben-xvi_let_20070707_lettera-vescovi.html .

The Mass in the Extraordinary form is a treasure for the Church and a compass by which to judge all modern liturgical issues.

CHAPTER 49

Obedience Revisited

a/k/a

Is a Small Disobedience Unimportant?

Observation one day: Yesterday I was moving some donated books out of the classroom, when I briefly opened a little book of quotes of St. Josemaría Escrivá and these words stared up at me: "In apostolic work there is no such thing as a trifling disobedience." This morning I opened St. Josemaría's little book to re-read the quote I read yesterday. In addition, I noticed this quote:

> *The enemy: "Will you obey,*
> *even in this ridiculous little detail?"*
>
> *You with God's grace: "I will obey,*
> *even in this <u>heroic</u> little detail!"*

CHAPTER 50

Discomfort in Being Rich Among the Poor

a/k/a

What Jesus Said About the Poor

Question: We are here at an extravagant resort, extremely elegant and quite expensive, babysitting some of our grandchildren while our daughter and son-in-law attend a homeschool conference. We took the kids to the pool and spent a few hours there, then went up to the room to play and spend time with them. We all had a lot of fun. The thing is, Father, I kept noticing the difference between those who worked there cleaning rooms—mostly black and Hispanic—and the opulent wealth of those who were staying at the resort—mostly white—and I felt uncomfortable. I always wonder why it must be so that some people have so much money and others are so poor. And then I wonder what I am to do about it.

Father Jeffry: Remember that you can't change something that is bigger than society itself. Christ said, "You will always have the poor." Look at it this way, because these rich people go to hotels like this, they give jobs to the poor! Even people who play golf and drive fancy sports cars create jobs. Look at all the restaurant jobs.

CHAPTER 51

Cutting Corners

a/k/a

Sleep (7 months later): The Final Round

Question: On Wednesday morning, I was in the chapel, and the verse came to mind that says something like, "Probe me and know my heart. Try me and know my thoughts. And then fix whatever is wrong in me so that I will be faithful." Something like that. So, I prayed that prayer to Jesus in the Blessed Sacrament. Then later in the day, I was tutoring, and I was sooo sleepy. I had skipped my nap--I don't remember why--so I struggled to stay alert. That night when I went to bed, it was 10:17 and I still hadn't turned off the light. I thought, "It's not that far from 10:00." But then it came to me that I had been doing that for a while. I remembered that sometimes it was 10:30 and maybe later than that, but I don't think so. And then I said to God, "But it's the 'spirit' of the law, right?", but that didn't settle well. And when I did the examen after turning out the light, I understood that I was not following the spirit of this guideline. The spirit of this was God's desire that I should get proper rest, and I was not doing that. Instead, I was cutting corners and undermining the spirit of the law. And so I was tired and not my best for my students or my family.

At Mass this morning, I thought about how "the spirit of the law" ends up having to be "the letter of the law" for me because I tend to cut corners. Is "cutting corners" a sin, Father? It feels like it is and that the Holy Spirit is trying to correct me, but I've never seen a sin like that listed in any Examination of Conscience.

Father Jeffry: Apparently, you've allowed a concept to enter into your daily schedule... "spirit". The spirit of a law could be interpreted in any way by anybody to suit them. "Be in bed with the lights out at 10:00 pm is not a spirit-filled duty. It's a fulfillment thing... Either you do it or you don't. If you don't, your soul, with its intellectual ability, convicts you. That seems to be the case. You don't cut corners on duties and still fulfill them. Other things you can, e.g., store-bought pasta, instead of homemade pasta.

One more thing... Don't regard yourself as one who is disobedient. Look at yourself as one with whom God is well pleased because of all you do to be the person He wants you to be! Carry on.

Reply (*after prayer*): I'm sorry I broke my word to you during those several days of not going to bed at 10:00. I didn't exactly mean to disobey, but I didn't exactly mean *not* to disobey either. I do understand that, as the result of going to bed late, I went against God's will for me that I get proper rest and be able to do my best for God, for others, and myself.

Note: This time the lesson finally stuck!

CHAPTER 52

Happy Obedience

a/k/a

Journaling with Joy!

This thought came to me one day: *How many times a day I obey Father Jeffry as my spiritual director in Christ, especially regarding the phone, sleep, prayer, and vocation! And how happy I am in that obedience!*

I wrote that thought in my journal.

◆◆◆

CHAPTER 53

P.S. on Sleep

a/k/a

What If I Go to Bed an Hour Earlier Sometimes?

Question: I have a question to ask you. I have been in bed with lights out no later 10:00 p.m. since May 13th <u>every night</u>--no exceptions. It really wasn't hard. I just had do make up my mind to do it. Well, now what I'm wondering is this: If I were to go to bed with lights out by 9:00 p.m. on a particular night, could I get up the next morning at 4:00 in order to write from 4:00-5:00 a.m.? The house would be quiet at 4:00 and so I wouldn't be interrupted like I am during the day. At 5:00, I would have coffee and pray Morning Prayer and do my spiritual reading, and then I would go to the Adoration Chapel at 5:45. Would that be good, Father? Or would it be better if I stick with the same bedtime and wake up time every day in order to stay on track, since it has been such a struggle to get to this point?

I'm sorry I'm such a child on this issue. Either way, I will do what you recommend.

Father Jeffry: The important aspect of the schedule is the regularity in going to bed and waking. It might be harder going to bed earlier. As you like. Also, I would have coffee while I write.

Reply...(*later*): I decided to stick with 10-5 for sleep. Why? 1) Because I don't think I would get to bed by 9:00 every night, but just on some nights, and so my sleep would no longer be consistent, and 2) When I tentatively brought up the idea to George, he wasn't too keen on it. I have come to realize that I put him through a lot of upset in previous years by staying up to all hours, not coming to bed or being out of bed, and by pushing my body too hard and being tense and tired. I love George very much, and I want to be considerate of him in this. So, I will continue to be in bed with lights out by 10:00 and stay in bed until 5:00.

◆◆◆

CHAPTER 54

Vocation

a/k/a

The Joy of Knowing What to Do with My Time

Question: Father Jeffry, I have noticed something this week. I don't feel "squirrelly" anymore, wandering from task to task while wondering what I should really be doing. Instead, I have in mind my vocation and current mission:

1) Write for the glory of God.

2) Read one book at a time (audiobooks aside) so that I have time to write.

3) Teach my students well, both in tutoring and at Faith Formation;

4) Take care of my mother and assume authority, making decisions for her when she is indecisive or confused;

5) Live fully my vocation as wife and mother with joy and dedication!

I am still being faithful to sleeping 10-5 and praying Morning Prayer, Evening Prayer, the Rosary, the Divine Mercy Chaplet, and intercessory prayers every day for you and for others.

Have a blessed, beautiful, bountiful day, Father!
Kathleen

Books Read During These 2+ Years

Mother Teresa, CEO
by Ruma Bose and Lou Faust

Abandonment to Divine Providence
by Jean-Pierre de Caussade

The Intellectual Life
by A.G. Sertillanges, O.P.

For Women Only: what you need to know about the inner lives of men
by Shaunti Feldhahn

Saint Anthony and the Christ Child
by Helen Walker Homan

The Fulfillment of All Desire
by Ralph Martin

Deep Conversion/Deep Prayer
by Thomas Dubay, S.M.

The Curé of Ars
by Milton Lomask

Praying for Your Husband from Head to Toe
by Sharon Jaynes

Trustful Surrender to Divine Providence
by Father Jean Baptiste Saint-Jure and
Blessed Claude de la Colombière

Stepping on the Serpent: The Journey of Trust with Mary
by Fr. Thaddaeus Lancton, MIC

To Light a Fire on the Earth
by Robert Barron with John L. Allen, Jr.

Challenges Makes Champions
by Fr. Cedric Pisegna, C.P.

The Gold of Exodus
by Howard Blum

Consoling Thoughts on Trials of an Interior Life
by Saint Francis de Sales, compiled by Pere Huguet

True Devotion to Mary
by Saint Louis de Montfort, adapted by Eddie Doherty

*Inside the Atheist Mind: Unmasking the Religion of Those
Who Say There Is No God*
by Anthony DeStefano

Lord of the World
by Robert Hugh Benson

Autobiography of Gemma Galgani
by Saint Gemma Galgani

Lessons in Hope
by George Weigel

Introduction to the Devout Life
by Saint Francis de Sales

The Road to Cana
by Anne Rice

ABOUT THE AUTHOR

Kathleen M. Alford is a retired educator who now works as a tutor and writer. She lives in DeLand, Florida, with her husband, George, who is an avid surfer and beach evangelist. Together they have nine children and 21 grandchildren. In her spare time, Kathleen enjoys spending time with the kids and grandkids, as well as gardening, reading, crocheting, and swimming. And someday she hopes to follow her childhood dream of becoming a missionary!

ABOUT THE PRIEST

Father Jeffry Moore is a Roman Catholic priest and president of Women Here and Now (Mujeres Aquí y Ahora a/k/a MAYA), a humanitarian organization of volunteers dedicated to the economic empowerment of women in vulnerable communities. Goals of the project include improved telecommunications, pest control, medical care and nutrition, needed air transport, clean water, and sustainable food production (aquaponics and rabbit farming). MAYA is currently based in Panamá, but plans exist to extend the project to Colombia and other Latin American countries. For more information about the work and ministry of Women Here and Now, visit WomenHereandNow.org.

FATHER, CAN YOU TEACH ME HOW TO LIVE?

Made in the
USA
Columbia, SC